Christmas
COOKIES

Oxmoor House®

Copyright 1986 by Oxmoor House, Inc.
Book Division of Southern Progress Corporation
P.O. Box 2463, Birmingham, Alabama 35201

Recipes adapted from *Southern Living®* cookbooks. *Southern Living®* is a federally registered trademark belonging to Southern Living, Inc.

Library of Congress Catalog Number: 86-60695

ISBN: 0-8487-0701-X

Manufactured in the United States of America

Second Printing 1987

CHRISTMAS COOKIES Cookbook

Book Editor: Ellen W. de Lathouder
Editorial Assistant: Karen Parris
Designer and Illustrator: Yukie McLean
Photographer: Jim Bathie
Food Stylist: Sara Jane Ball

Cover (left to right from top): *Chocolate-Mint Layer Squares (page 5), Gingerbread Cookies (page 42), Greek Holiday Cookies (page 80), Candy Cane Cookies (74), Bourbon Balls (page 60), Chocolate Chip Forgotten Cookies (page 23), Holly Squares (page 16), Basic Pressed Cookies (page 74), and Linzer Cookies (page 47).*

CONTENTS

INTRODUCTION

Christmastime is cookie time! Brown-suited gingerbread men with raisins for buttons and icing for hair; red-and green-sugared Christmas trees and Santas posing as delectable ornaments; cookies flavored with bourbon and coconut before they are shaped into balls and rolled in sugar; date-filled, lemon-filled, and jelly-filled cookies; and perennial favorites, such as brownies and chocolate chip cookies, are truly the makings of Christmas cheer.

But the fun really begins with the baking—when the rolling pin and flour bin, mixing bowls and cookie sheets, pecans and candied fruit, sprinkles and spices are assembled, and when the eager helpers, young and old, assemble on their own. What is more homey than a kitchen filled with apron-clad children and the aroma of warm cookies? More productive than a cheerful assembly line making cookies for holiday entertainment and gift giving? More heartwarming than a gift of homemade Christmas cookies?

Recipes innovative and worthy of gift giving abound in this unique collection. *Christmas Cookies* offers American favorites—those recipes that evoke, "It wouldn't be Christmas without Grandma's fruitcake cookies," while foreign specialties highlight the universal appeal of holiday cookies. Many of the recipes leave room for the imaginative cook to create her own seasonal masterpieces. And when the season is over, this cookbook will serve as a valuable resource for delicious cookies that will give pleasure the year-round.

The recipes are organized according to the method of preparation. If the cookies are baked in a pan and cut into bars or squares, that's where you'll find them, in "Bars and Squares." Cookies made of dough dropped from a spoon onto a cookie sheet are "Drop Cookies." When the dough is rolled out and cut with a cutter or chilled and then sliced with a knife, the recipe appears in "Rolled and Sliced Cookies." "Shaped Cookies" are shaped by hand or cookie press. The methods all come together in the final chapter where an array of "Foreign Cookies" takes shape.

BARS AND SQUARES

DUTCH BUTTER SQUARES

1 cup butter, softened
1 cup sugar
1 egg
2 cups all-purpose
    flour

Cream butter in a large mixing bowl; gradually add sugar, beating until light and fluffy. Add egg, and beat well. Gradually stir in flour, blending well. (Dough will be sticky.)

Divide dough in half. Place each portion of dough in a well-greased 8-inch square pan. With floured hands, press dough evenly into pans.

Place pans in a cold oven. Bake at 350° for 20 minutes or until lightly browned. Remove from oven, and cut into 2-inch squares while warm. Remove from pans, and cool on wire racks. Yield: about 2½ dozen.

ALMOND SHORTBREAD

1 cup butter, softened
1 cup sugar
1 egg yolk
1 teaspoon almond extract
2 cups all-purpose
    flour
1 cup blanched almonds, finely
    ground

Cream butter in a large mixing bowl; gradually add sugar, beating until light and fluffy. Add egg yolk; beat well. Stir in almond extract. Gradually add flour and ground almonds, stirring until well blended.

Press dough into a lightly greased 13- x 9- x 2-inch baking pan. Bake at 325° for 40 minutes or until lightly browned. Cut into 2-inch squares while warm. Cool in pan 10 minutes, and remove to a wire rack to cool completely. Yield: about 2 dozen.

ALMOND SQUARES

1 cup butter
¾ cup sugar
1 egg, separated
½ cup almond paste
1 teaspoon almond extract
2 cups all-purpose
    flour
1 (2½-ounce) package sliced
    almonds

Cream butter in a large mixing bowl; gradually add sugar, beating until light and fluffy. Add egg yolk, almond paste, and flavoring; beat until well blended. Stir in flour.

Spread mixture in a 13- x 9- x 2-inch baking pan. Beat egg white (at room temperature) until foamy; brush over entire surface of dough, and sprinkle with almonds. Bake at 350° for 35 minutes or until lightly browned. Cool thoroughly, and cut into 2-inch squares. Store in airtight containers. Yield: about 2 dozen.

NATCHEZ BARS

1 cup unsalted butter
1 cup sugar
1 egg, separated
2 cups all-purpose flour
  Grated rind of ½ lemon
  Juice of ½ lemon
1 cup chopped pecans or
  walnuts

Cream butter in a large mixing bowl; add sugar, beating until light and fluffy. Add egg yolk, flour, lemon rind, and juice; mix well.

Press dough evenly into an ungreased 15- x 10- x 1-inch jellyroll pan. Brush with lightly beaten egg white; sprinkle with pecans. Bake at 325° for 25 to 30 minutes. Cut into 3- x 1-inch bars while warm. Remove to wire racks to cool. Yield: about 4 dozen.

FROSTED FUDGE SQUARES

3½ (1-ounce) squares unsweetened
  chocolate
¾ cup butter or margarine
4 eggs
2 cups sugar
½ teaspoon salt
1 teaspoon vanilla extract
1 cup all-purpose
  flour
1½ cups chopped pecans or
  walnuts
  Favorite Brownie Frosting

Melt chocolate and butter in top of a double boiler over simmering water; set aside to cool.

Beat egg whites lightly with a wooden spoon; gradually add sugar, salt, and vanilla, stirring well. Stir in cooled chocolate mixture.

Sift flour over pecans; mix well, and stir into batter. Spread batter in a greased 12- x 8- x 2-inch baking pan. Bake at 325° for 35 to 40 minutes. Frost with Favorite Brownie Frosting, and cut into 1½-inch squares while warm. Yield: about 3 dozen.

Favorite Brownie Frosting:

1½ (1-ounce) squares unsweetened
  chocolate
2 tablespoons butter or margarine
¼ cup whipping cream
⅓ cup firmly packed dark brown
  sugar
  Dash of salt
½ teaspoon vanilla extract
½ teaspoon sherry extract
1½ cups sifted powdered sugar

Combine chocolate, butter, whipping cream, brown sugar, and salt in a small saucepan. Bring mixture to a boil, stirring constantly until chocolate melts. Remove from heat; add flavorings and enough powdered sugar to yield desired spreading consistency. Yield: frosting for about 3 dozen squares.

Note: For a quick frosting, place 8 small, thin milk chocolate bars over warm brownies; cover with a flat pan for a few minutes to hasten melting. Remove pan, and spread chocolate evenly over surface.

JIFFY CHOCOLATE BARS

½ cup all-purpose flour
½ cup sugar
¼ teaspoon salt
⅓ cup vegetable oil
1 egg
2 tablespoons milk
1 (1-ounce) square unsweetened
  chocolate, melted
½ teaspoon vanilla extract
½ cup finely chopped pecans

Combine flour, sugar, and salt in a medium mixing bowl. Combine oil, egg, milk, melted chocolate, and vanilla in a small mixing bowl, stirring well. Make a well in center of flour mixture; add oil mixture, and mix until smooth.

Spread batter evenly in a 15- x 10- x 1-inch jellyroll pan. Sprinkle pecans over batter. Bake at 400° for 10 minutes or until set. Cut into 2½- x 1½-inch bars while warm. Yield: about 3 dozen.

CHOCOLATE-FILLED SQUARES

¾ **cup finely chopped walnuts**
3 **tablespoons all-purpose**
   flour
3 **tablespoons sugar**
3 **tablespoons butter or margarine,**
   softened
½ **cup butter or margarine**
1 **cup sugar**
3 **eggs**
2 **(1-ounce) squares unsweetened**
   chocolate, melted
1 **teaspoon vanilla**
   extract
⅓ **cup all-purpose flour**
½ **teaspoon baking**
   powder
⅛ **teaspoon salt**

Combine first 3 ingredients. Add softened butter, blending well. Press into an ungreased 9-inch square baking pan.

Combine next 8 ingredients in a large bowl. Beat at low speed of an electric mixer until smooth; pour over flour mixture. Bake at 325° for 35 to 40 minutes; cool in pan. Cut into 1-inch squares. Yield: about 7 dozen.

CHOCOLATE DREAM BROWNIES

1 **cup shortening**
4 **(1-ounce) squares unsweetened**
   chocolate
2 **cups sugar**
4 **eggs, beaten**
1 **teaspoon vanilla**
   extract
1½ **cups all-purpose flour**
½ **teaspoon salt**
1 **cup chopped pecans**
   Frosting (recipe follows)
   Finely chopped pecans
   (optional)

Melt shortening and chocolate in top of a double boiler over simmering water.

Remove from heat; add sugar, mixing well. Add eggs and vanilla, beating until well blended. Add flour and salt, stirring well. Fold in 1 cup pecans.

Spread batter evenly in a well-greased 13- x 9- x 2-inch baking pan. Bake at 400° for 20 minutes. Let cool completely in pan.

Spread frosting evenly over brownies, and sprinkle with finely chopped pecans, if desired. Allow frosting to set before cutting brownies into 3- x 2-inch bars or assorted shapes. Yield: about 1½ dozen.

Frosting:

2 **(1-ounce) squares unsweetened**
   chocolate
3 **tablespoons water**
1 **tablespoon butter or margarine,**
   softened
2 **cups sifted powdered sugar**
½ **teaspoon vanilla extract**
1 **egg, beaten**

Combine chocolate and water in top of a double boiler; cook over simmering water, stirring constantly, until chocolate melts.

Remove from heat; stir in butter. Cool slightly. Gradually add remaining ingredients, beating until smooth. Use immediately. Yield: frosting for about 1½ dozen bars.

BROWNIE CHEWS

⅓ **cup shortening**
2 **(1-ounce) squares unsweetened**
   chocolate
2 **eggs, well beaten**
1 **cup sugar**
1½ **cups quick-cooking or regular**
   oats, uncooked
½ **teaspoon baking powder**
¼ **teaspoon salt**
1 **teaspoon vanilla extract**
½ **cup chopped pecans**
   Sifted powdered sugar

Melt shortening and chocolate in top of a double boiler over simmering water.

Combine eggs and sugar; beat well. Stir in oats, baking powder, salt, vanilla, and pecans. Add chocolate mixture; stir well. Spread batter in a greased 8-inch square baking pan. Bake at 350° for 25 minutes. Cool; dust with powdered sugar, and cut into 1½-inch squares. Yield: about 2 dozen.

CHOCOLATE-MINT LAYER SQUARES

2 (1-ounce) squares unsweetened
   chocolate
½ cup butter or margarine
2 eggs
1 cup sugar
½ cup all-purpose flour
½ cup chopped walnuts or pecans
1½ cups sifted powdered sugar
3 tablespoons butter or margarine,
   softened
2 tablespoons whipping cream
¾ teaspoon peppermint extract
2 drops green food coloring
   (optional)
2 (1-ounce) squares sweet baking
   chocolate
2 tablespoons butter or margarine
1 teaspoon vanilla extract

Melt unsweetened chocolate and ½ cup butter in top of a double boiler over simmering water; cool.

Combine eggs and 1 cup sugar, beating until light and fluffy; stir in flour, walnuts, and cooled chocolate. Spread mixture in a greased 9-inch square baking pan. Bake at 350° for 25 minutes. Cool in pan on a wire rack.

Combine powdered sugar, 3 tablespoons butter, whipping cream, and peppermint extract. Stir in food coloring, if desired. Beat until smooth. Spread evenly over baked layer; cover and chill 1 hour or until firm.

Melt sweet chocolate and 2 tablespoons butter in top of a double boiler over simmering water; stir in vanilla, and drizzle over peppermint layer. Cover and chill 1 hour or until firm. Cut into 1-inch squares. Yield: about 7 dozen.

GERMAN CREAM CHEESE BROWNIES

1 (4-ounce) package sweet baking
   chocolate
¼ cup plus 1 tablespoon butter,
   softened and divided
3 eggs, divided
1 cup sugar, divided
1½ teaspoons vanilla extract, divided
¼ teaspoon almond extract
½ cup plus 1 tablespoon
   all-purpose flour, divided
½ teaspoon baking powder
¼ teaspoon salt
½ cup coarsely chopped pecans
1 (3-ounce) package cream cheese,
   softened

Melt chocolate and 3 tablespoons butter in top of a double boiler over simmering water, stirring constantly. Let cool.

Beat 2 eggs in a medium mixing bowl until light and fluffy; gradually add ¾ cup sugar, beating until thick and lemon colored. Add 1 teaspoon vanilla and almond extract, stirring well.

Combine ½ cup flour, baking powder, and salt; gradually add to egg mixture, stirring well. Stir in reserved chocolate mixture and pecans. Pour batter into a well-greased 9-inch square baking pan, reserving 1 cup batter.

Cream remaining 2 tablespoons butter and cream cheese in a medium mixing bowl; gradually add remaining ¼ cup sugar, beating until light and fluffy. Add 1 egg; beat well. Add remaining flour and vanilla, stirring well. Spread evenly over chocolate batter in pan.

Drop reserved batter by tablespoonfuls onto cream cheese batter; swirl to marble. Bake at 350° for 45 minutes or until lightly browned. Cool; cut into 1½-inch squares. Yield: 3 dozen.

GERMAN CHOCOLATE BROWNIES

2 eggs, lightly beaten
1 cup sugar
1 (4-ounce) package sweet baking
   chocolate, melted
¾ cup all-purpose flour
¾ cup chopped pecans
½ cup butter or margarine, melted
1 teaspoon vanilla extract
   Frosting (recipe follows)

Combine eggs and sugar; beat well. Add slightly cooled chocolate, flour, pecans, butter, and vanilla; beat well. Spread batter in a greased 9-inch square baking pan. Bake at 350° for 40 minutes. Cool completely in pan. Spread frosting evenly over brownies, and cut into 1½-inch squares. Yield: 3 dozen.

Frosting:

½ cup evaporated milk
½ cup sugar
¼ cup butter or margarine
2 egg yolks, lightly beaten
½ teaspoon vanilla extract
½ cup chopped pecans
⅓ cup flaked coconut

Combine milk, sugar, butter, and egg yolks in a medium saucepan; cook over medium heat. Stir until thickened. Remove from heat, and stir in vanilla, pecans, and coconut. Cool completely. Yield: frosting for 3 dozen squares.

CREAM BARS

¾ cup butter or margarine,
   softened
¼ cup firmly packed light brown
   sugar
¼ cup firmly packed dark brown
   sugar
1½ cups all-purpose flour
1 (16-ounce) carton commercial
   sour cream
1 tablespoon plus 1½ teaspoons
   sugar
1½ teaspoons vanilla extract
   Red maraschino cherries, halved

Cream butter; add brown sugar, beating until light and fluffy. Add flour; mix well. Press mixture into an ungreased 13- x 9- x 2-inch baking pan. Bake at 350° for 25 minutes.

Combine sour cream, 1 tablespoon plus 1½ teaspoons sugar, and vanilla; beat well. Spread over baked mixture. Bake at 350° for 10 minutes. Cool in pan. Cut into 3- x 1½-inch bars; remove from pan, and place a cherry half in center of each bar. Yield: about 2 dozen.

CHEWY BAR COOKIES

½ cup butter or margarine
1 cup firmly packed light brown
   sugar
1 cup firmly packed dark brown
   sugar
2 eggs
1½ cups all-purpose flour
1½ teaspoons baking powder
½ teaspoon salt
1 teaspoon vanilla
1 cup chopped pecans

Cream butter; gradually add sugar, beating well. Add eggs, beating well.

Combine flour, baking powder, and salt; add to creamed mixture, stirring well. Stir in vanilla and pecans. Spread in a greased 13- x 9- x 2-inch baking pan. Bake at 325° for 30 minutes. Cut into 2- x 1-inch bars; cool on wire racks. Yield: about 4½ dozen.

PEANUT BUTTER BROWNIES

½ cup smooth or chunky peanut
   butter
⅓ cup butter or margarine
⅔ cup sugar
½ cup firmly packed dark brown
   sugar
2 eggs
½ teaspoon almond extract
1 cup all-purpose flour
1 teaspoon baking powder
¼ teaspoon salt

Combine peanut butter and butter, blending well. Gradually add sugar, beating until light and fluffy. Add eggs, beating well. Stir in almond extract.

Combine flour, baking powder, and salt. Add to creamed mixture; stir well. Spread mixture evenly in a greased 9-inch square pan. Bake at 350° for 30 to 35 minutes. Cool completely in pan, and cut into 1½-inch squares. Yield: 3 dozen.

BUTTERSCOTCH BROWNIES

2 (6-ounce) packages butterscotch morsels
½ cup butter or margarine
4 eggs
1 cup firmly packed brown sugar
1½ cups all-purpose flour
1 teaspoon baking powder
1¼ teaspoons salt
2 cups chopped pecans

Melt butterscotch morsels and butter in top of a double boiler over simmering water; remove from heat.

Combine eggs and sugar, beating until light and fluffy.

Sift together flour, baking powder, and salt; add to creamed mixture, stirring well. Stir in butterscotch mixture and pecans. Pour mixture into a lightly greased 15- x 10- x 1-inch jellyroll pan. Bake at 350° for 25 minutes. Cool completely in pan, and cut into 2-inch squares. Store in airtight containers. Yield: about 3 dozen.

ALMOND MOCHA BARS

1 cup butter, margarine, or shortening
1 cup firmly packed brown sugar
1 teaspoon almond extract
2¼ cups all-purpose flour
1 teaspoon instant coffee granules
½ teaspoon baking powder
¼ teaspoon salt
1 (6-ounce) package semisweet chocolate morsels
½ cup chopped almonds

Cream butter in a large mixing bowl; gradually add brown sugar, mixing well. Stir in almond extract.

Combine flour, coffee, baking powder, and salt. Add to creamed mixture, stirring until thoroughly blended. Add chocolate morsels and chopped almonds, blending well. Press dough evenly into a greased 15- x 10- x 1-inch jellyroll pan. Bake at 375° for 25 to 30 minutes. Cut into 3- x 1-inch bars while warm. Cool completely, and store in airtight containers. Yield: about 4 dozen.

CHIPPER DATE BROWNIES

1 (8-ounce) package pitted dates, chopped
1 cup boiling water
1 cup shortening
1 cup sugar
2 eggs
1 teaspoon vanilla extract
1¾ cups all-purpose flour
¼ cup cocoa
½ teaspoon baking soda
½ teaspoon salt
¾ cup chopped walnuts
1 (6-ounce) package semisweet chocolate morsels

Combine dates and boiling water in a small mixing bowl; cool to room temperature.

Cream shortening in a large mixing bowl; gradually add sugar, beating well. Add eggs, beating well. Stir in vanilla and date mixture, mixing well.

Combine flour, cocoa, soda, and salt in a medium mixing bowl. Add to creamed mixture, stirring well. Spread batter in a greased 15- x 10- x 1-inch jellyroll pan; sprinkle with walnuts and chocolate morsels. Bake at 375° for 25 to 30 minutes. Cool completely in pan; cut into 2-inch squares. Yield: about 3 dozen.

CHOCOLATE-BUTTERSCOTCH SQUARES

½ cup butter or margarine
1 egg yolk
2 tablespoons water
½ teaspoon almond
   extract
1¼ cups all-purpose flour
1 tablespoon sugar
1 teaspoon baking
   powder
   Dash of salt
1 (6-ounce) package butterscotch
   morsels
1 (6-ounce) package semisweet
   chocolate morsels
   Topping (recipe follows)
1 cup finely ground pecans or
   walnuts

Combine butter, egg yolk, water, and almond extract in a large mixing bowl; beat at medium speed of an electric mixer until well blended.

Sift together flour, sugar, baking powder, and salt in a medium mixing bowl; add to butter mixture, blending well. Press dough into a greased 13- x 9- x 2-inch baking pan. Bake at 350° for 10 minutes; remove from oven, and immediately sprinkle butterscotch and chocolate morsels over top. Return to oven 4 to 5 minutes. Remove from oven, and smooth morsels evenly over pastry. Cover with topping, and sprinkle with pecans. Bake an additional 30 to 35 minutes. Cool and cut into 1½-inch squares. Store in airtight containers. Yield: about 4 dozen.

Topping:

2 eggs, beaten
¾ cup sugar
¼ cup plus 2 tablespoons butter or
   margarine, melted
1 teaspoon vanilla extract
½ teaspoon almond extract

Combine all ingredients in a medium mixing bowl; mix well. Yield: topping for about 4 dozen squares.

CHOCOLATE CHIP TOFFEE GRAHAMS

11 whole graham crackers (4½ x 2¼
   inches),
   broken into squares
1 cup butter or margarine
1 cup sugar
1 teaspoon ground cinnamon
½ cup finely chopped pecans
1 (6-ounce) package semisweet
   chocolate mini-morsels

Arrange graham cracker squares in a single layer in a 15- x 10- x 1-inch jellyroll pan. Set aside.

Combine butter and sugar in a medium saucepan. Cook over medium heat, stirring until butter melts. Bring to a boil; boil 2 minutes. Remove from heat; stir in cinnamon and pecans. Pour mixture over graham crackers, spreading evenly to edges of pan. Bake at 350° for 10 to 12 minutes. Sprinkle with chocolate morsels. Cool 5 minutes; separate cookies, and transfer to waxed paper-lined cookie sheets, using a spatula. Refrigerate until chocolate hardens. Store cookies between layers of waxed paper in an airtight container in refrigerator. Yield: about 2 dozen.

CHOCOLATE-FROSTED TOFFEE BARS

1 cup butter
1 cup firmly packed brown
   sugar
1 egg yolk
½ teaspoon vanilla extract
2 cups all-purpose flour
1 (6-ounce) package semisweet
   chocolate morsels, melted
1 cup finely chopped pecans,
   toasted

Cream butter in a medium mixing bowl; gradually add sugar, beating until light and fluffy. Add egg yolk and vanilla, beating until well blended. Add flour, blending well. Press dough evenly into an ungreased 15- x 10- x 1-inch jellyroll pan. Bake at 325° for 20 minutes or until lighly browned. Cool slightly, and spread with melted chocolate. Sprinkle with pecans, and cut into 2- x 1-inch bars. Cool completely on wire racks. Yield: about 6 dozen.

CONGO SQUARES

2½ cups all-purpose flour, sifted
1½ teaspoons baking powder
½ teaspoon salt
⅔ cup butter or margarine
2¼ cups firmly packed brown
    sugar
3 eggs
2 teaspoons fresh lemon juice
1 cup chopped pecans
1 (6-ounce) package semisweet
    chocolate morsels

Sift together flour, baking powder, and salt in a large mixing bowl.

Melt butter in a large saucepan; remove from heat. Stir in sugar; add eggs, one at a time, beating well after each addition. Add lemon juice, flour mixture, pecans, and chocolate morsels; blend well. Spread batter in a greased 12- x 8- x 2-inch baking pan. Bake at 350° for 25 to 30 minutes. (Do not overbake.) Cut into 1½-inch squares while warm, and cool completely in pan. Yield: about 3 dozen.

PENUCHE SQUARES

¼ cup shortening
1 cup firmly packed brown
    sugar
1 egg
1 teaspoon vanilla extract
1 cup all-purpose flour
1 teaspoon baking powder
¼ teaspoon salt
1 (6-ounce) package semisweet
    chocolate or butterscotch
    morsels
½ cup chopped pecans

Melt shortening, and pour into a large mixing bowl to cool slightly; add brown sugar, beating well. Add egg and vanilla, beating until light and fluffy.

Combine flour, baking powder, and salt in a small mixing bowl; add to creamed mixture. Gently stir in chocolate or butterscotch morsels and pecans. Spread mixture evenly in a greased 8-inch square baking pan. Bake at 350° for 25 to 30 minutes. (Do not overbake.) Cool completely in pan, and cut into 1-inch squares. Yield: about 5 dozen.

CROESUS SQUARES

1 cup butter or margarine
½ cup sugar
⅔ cup firmly packed brown
    sugar
3 eggs, separated
1 tablespoon water
1 teaspoon vanilla extract
½ teaspoon almond extract
2 cups sifted all-purpose flour
¼ teaspoon baking soda
½ teaspoon salt
1 (12-ounce) package semisweet
    chocolate morsels
1 cup chopped black walnuts or
    pecans
    Dash of cream of tartar
½ cup firmly packed brown sugar

Combine butter, ½ cup sugar, and ⅔ cup brown sugar in a large mixing bowl. Beat at medium speed of an electric mixer until blended. Beat egg yolks lightly, and add to creamed mixture. Add water and flavorings, beating well.

Sift together flour, soda, and salt. Stir into creamed mixture; blend well. Spread batter in an ungreased 15- x 10- x 1-inch jellyroll pan. Sprinkle with chocolate and walnuts.

Beat egg whites (at room temperature) until foamy; add cream of tartar, beating until stiff peaks form. Fold in ½ cup brown sugar; spread over chocolate morsels and walnuts. Bake at 300° for 50 to 55 minutes. Cool in pan; cut into 2-inch squares. Yield: about 3 dozen.

ANGEL SQUARES

½ cup shortening
1 cup sugar
1 egg
1 egg yolk
¾ teaspoon vanilla extract, divided
1½ cups all-purpose flour
2 teaspoons baking powder
½ teaspoon salt
1 egg white
1 cup firmly packed brown
    sugar
⅓ cup chopped pecans

Cream shortening in a large mixing bowl; gradually add 1 cup sugar, beating well. Add egg and egg yolk, beating well. Stir in ¼ teaspoon vanilla.

Combine flour, baking powder, and salt; gradually add to creamed mixture, stirring well. Spread mixture in a greased 11- x 7- x 1-inch jellyroll pan.

Beat egg white (at room temperature) until foamy. Gradually add brown sugar, beating until stiff peaks form. Add remaining ½ teaspoon vanilla. Spread evenly over mixture in pan, and sprinkle with pecans. Bake at 325° for 25 minutes or until lightly browned. Cool and cut into 2-inch squares. Yield: about 1½ dozen.

APPLE SPICE BARS

½ cup shortening
1 cup sugar
3 eggs, beaten
1 cup all-purpose flour
1 teaspoon baking powder
½ teaspoon salt
1 teaspoon ground cinnamon
½ teaspoon ground nutmeg
¼ teaspoon ground cloves
1 cup regular oats, uncooked
1½ cups chopped, peeled apple
½ cup raisins
½ cup chopped pecans
    Sifted powdered sugar

Cream shortening; add 1 cup sugar, beating well. Add eggs; beat well.

Sift together flour, baking powder, salt, and spices in a medium mixing bowl; gradually add to creamed mixture, stirring well. Stir in oats, apple, raisins, and pecans, mixing well.

Press mixture into a greased 15- x 10- x 1-inch jellyroll pan. Bake at 350° for 25 minutes or until lightly browned. Cool on a wire rack; sprinkle with powdered sugar, and cut into 2- x 1-inch bars. Yield: about 6 dozen.

APRICOT BLONDIES

½ cup shortening
1 cup firmly packed brown sugar
2 eggs
1½ teaspoons vanilla extract
1¾ cups all-purpose flour
2 teaspoons baking powder
½ teaspoon salt
1 cup chopped dried apricots
½ cup chopped pecans

Cream shortening; add sugar, beating well. Add eggs; beat well. Stir in vanilla.

Combine flour, baking powder, and salt; add to creamed mixture, mixing well. Fold in apricots and pecans. Press mixture into a greased 13- x 9- x 2-inch baking pan. Bake at 350° for 18 to 20 minutes. Cool; cut into 2- x 1-inch bars. Yield: about 4½ dozen.

APRICOT BARS

1½ cups sifted all-purpose flour
1 teaspoon baking powder
¼ teaspoon salt
1½ cups quick-cooking oats,
    uncooked
1 cup firmly packed brown sugar
¾ cup butter or margarine
¾ cup apricot preserves or jam

Combine flour, baking powder, and salt; stir in oats and sugar. Cut in butter with a pastry blender until mixture resembles coarse meal.

Press two-thirds of mixture into an ungreased 11- x 7- x 1-inch jellyroll pan.

Spread preserves over surface; sprinkle with remaining oats mixture. Bake at 350° for 30 to 35 minutes. Cool; cut into 3- x 1-inch bars. Yield: about 2 dozen.

APRICOT SQUARES

⅔ cup dried apricots
½ cup butter or margarine, softened
¼ cup sugar
1⅓ cups all purpose flour, divided
½ teaspoon baking powder
¼ teaspoon salt
1 cup firmly packed brown sugar
2 eggs, well beaten
½ teaspoon vanilla extract
½ cup chopped pecans

Rinse apricots, and place in a small saucepan with water to cover. Bring to a boil; boil 10 minutes. Drain; cool and chop. Set aside.

Combine butter, ¼ cup sugar, and 1 cup flour, blending well. Press mixture into a greased 8-inch square pan. Bake at 325° for 25 minutes.

Combine remaining ⅓ cup flour, baking powder, and salt in a small mixing bowl. Set aside.

Gradually add brown sugar to beaten eggs, beating well. Add reserved apricots, flour mixture, vanilla, and pecans. Spread evenly over baked crust. Bake at 325° for 30 minutes or until lightly browned. Cool in pan; cut into 2-inch squares. Yield: about 1½ dozen.

APRISCOTTIES

1¾ cups quick-cooking or regular oats, uncooked
1 cup all-purpose flour
1 cup firmly packed light brown sugar
1 teaspoon baking powder
1 teaspoon almond extract
½ cup butter or margarine
1 (12-ounce) jar (about 1 cup) apricot preserves

Combine oats, flour, sugar, baking powder, and almond extract in a large mixing bowl. Cut in butter with a pastry blender until mixture resembles coarse meal. Press 3 cups oats mixture firmly into a greased 9-inch square baking pan. Spread preserves evenly over oats mixture, leaving ¼-inch margin along sides. Top with remaining oats mixture. Bake at 375° for 25 to 30 minutes or until lightly browned. Cool on a wire rack; cut into 2-inch squares. Yield: about 1½ dozen.

LAYERED APRICOT SQUARES

1 cup all-purpose flour
⅓ cup sugar
½ cup butter
¾ cup chopped dried apricots
2 eggs
1 cup firmly packed brown sugar
⅓ cup all-purpose flour
½ teaspoon baking powder
¼ teaspoon salt
¼ teaspoon almond extract
¼ teaspoon vanilla extract
½ cup chopped walnuts
Sifted powdered sugar

Sift together 1 cup flour and ⅓ cup sugar in a medium mixing bowl; cut in butter with a pastry blender until mixture resembles coarse meal. Press into an ungreased 8-inch square baking pan. Bake at 350° for 30 minutes or until lightly browned. Set aside.

Place apricots in a small saucepan with water to cover; simmer 15 minutes. Drain; cool and chop. Set aside.

Beat eggs in a medium mixing bowl; gradually add brown sugar, beating well. Sift together ⅓ cup flour, baking powder, and salt in a small mixing bowl; add to egg mixture. Stir in reserved apricots, flavorings, and walnuts. Spread evenly over baked mixture. Bake at 350° for 30 to 35 minutes. Sprinkle with powdered sugar while warm; cool completely. Cut into 2-inch squares. Yield: about 1½ dozen.

BANANA SPICE BARS

1 small ripe banana, mashed
¼ cup shortening
1 egg
1 cup all-purpose flour
¾ cup sugar
½ teaspoon baking powder
¼ teaspoon baking soda
½ teaspoon salt
¾ teaspoon ground
    cinnamon
¼ teaspoon ground allspice
⅛ teaspoon ground cloves
¼ cup milk
⅓ cup chopped pecans
  Lemon Frosting

Combine banana and shortening; beat at high speed of an electric mixer 2 minutes. Add egg; beat 1 minute.

Sift together dry ingredients. Add to banana mixture; stir well. Stir in milk and pecans.

Pour batter into a greased 13- x 9- x 2-inch baking pan. Bake at 350° for 20 to 25 minutes. Spread with Lemon Frosting while warm; cool. Cut into 2- x 1½-inch bars. Yield: about 3 dozen.

Lemon Frosting:

1 cup sifted powdered sugar
2 tablespoons butter or margarine,
    melted
1 tablespoon water
2 tablespoons lemon juice

Combine sugar, butter, water, and lemon juice; beat until smooth. Yield: frosting for about 3 dozen bars.

CINNAMON BARS

1 cup butter or margarine,
    softened
1 cup sugar
1 egg, separated
2 cups sifted all-purpose flour
1 tablespoon plus 1 teaspoon
    ground cinnamon
1 cup chopped pecans

Cream butter in a large mixing bowl; add sugar, beating until light and fluffy. Add egg yolk, flour, and cinnamon; mix until well blended.

Press mixture into an ungreased 15- x 10- x 1-inch jellyroll pan; pour egg white over surface; drain off excess. Sprinkle chopped pecans over top; press lightly into dough. Bake at 325° for 25 to 30 minutes. Cut into 3- x 1-inch bars; cool on wire racks. Yield: about 4 dozen.

COCONUT DIAMONDS

½ cup butter, softened
1½ cups firmly packed brown sugar,
    divided
1 cup plus 2 tablespoons
    all-purpose flour, divided
1 teaspoon salt, divided
2 eggs, lightly beaten
1 teaspoon vanilla extract
1¼ cups flaked coconut
½ cup chopped pecans
  Lemon Frosting

Cream butter in a large mixing bowl; gradually add ½ cup brown sugar, beating until light and fluffy. Add 1 cup flour and ½ teaspoon salt, mixing well. Press mixture evenly into a 13- x 9- x 2-inch baking pan. Bake at 350° for 12 to 15 minutes.

Combine remaining ingredients, except Lemon Frosting, in a small mixing bowl. Spread evenly over baked mixture. Bake at 350° for 20 minutes or until lightly browned. Cool slightly; spread with Lemon Frosting. Cut into 2½-inch diamond shapes, and remove to wire racks to cool completely. Yield: 3 dozen.

Lemon Frosting:

¼ cup butter, softened
1½ cups sifted powdered sugar
2 teaspoons grated lemon rind
2 tablespoons fresh lemon juice

Combine all ingredients in small mixing bowl; beat until smooth. Yield: frosting for 3 dozen diamonds.

BLACK WALNUT-COCONUT BARS

1½ cups firmly packed brown sugar,
    divided
 1 cup plus 1 teaspoon all-purpose
    flour, divided
 ½ cup butter or margarine
 ¼ teaspoon salt
 2 eggs, beaten
 1 teaspoon vanilla
    extract
1½ cups flaked coconut
 1 cup chopped black walnuts

Combine ½ cup brown sugar and 1 cup flour in a medium mixing bowl; cut in butter with a pastry blender until mixture resembles coarse meal. Press dough evenly into a 9-inch square baking pan; bake at 375° for 10 minutes. Set aside to cool.

Combine 1 cup sugar, 1 teaspoon flour, salt, eggs, vanilla, coconut, and black walnuts in a medium mixing bowl. Pour over baked crust. Bake at 375° for 20 minutes. Remove to a wire rack to cool. Cut into 3- x 1½-inch bars. Yield: 1½ dozen.

COCONUT-CHOCOLATE MERINGUE BARS

 ¾ cup butter or margarine
 ½ cup sugar
1½ cups firmly packed brown sugar,
    divided
 3 eggs, separated
 1 teaspoon vanilla extract
 2 cups all-purpose flour
 1 teaspoon baking powder
 ¼ teaspoon baking soda
 ¼ teaspoon salt
 1 (6-ounce) package semisweet
    chocolate morsels
 1 cup flaked coconut
 ¾ cup coarsely chopped pecans

Combine butter, sugar, ½ cup brown sugar, egg yolks, and vanilla in a large mixing bowl; beat until thoroughly blended.

Combine flour, baking powder, soda, and salt in a medium mixing bowl. Add to creamed mixture; blend well. Press dough into a greased 13- x 9- x 2-inch baking pan; sprinkle with chocolate morsels, coconut, and pecans.

Beat egg whites (at room temperature) until foamy; gradually add remaining 1 cup brown sugar, beating until stiff peaks form. Spread meringue evenly over pecans. Bake at 350° for 35 to 40 minutes. Cool completely in pan; cut into 3- x 1-inch bars. Yield: about 3 dozen.

FROSTED COCONUT SQUARES

 1 cup plus 2 tablespoons
    all-purpose flour, divided
 ½ cup butter or margarine,
    softened
 2 eggs, lightly beaten
1½ cups firmly packed brown sugar
 ¼ teaspoon baking powder
 ½ teaspoon salt
 1 teaspoon vanilla extract
 ½ cup flaked coconut
1½ cups chopped pecans, divided
    Frosting (recipe follows)

Combine 1 cup flour and butter to make a smooth paste; spread evenly in a greased 9-inch square baking pan. Bake at 375° for 15 minutes.

Combine eggs, sugar, 2 tablespoons flour, baking powder, salt, and vanilla; blend well. Stir in coconut and 1 cup pecans; spread over warm crust. Bake at 375° for 20 minutes. Cool completely in pan; spread with frosting, and sprinkle with remaining pecans. Cut into 1½-inch squares. Yield: 3 dozen.

Frosting:

 2 tablespoons butter or margarine
 2 cups sifted powdered sugar
 2 tablespoons orange juice
 1 teaspoon fresh lemon juice

Combine all ingredients; beat with a wire whisk until smooth. Yield: frosting for 3 dozen squares.

LUSCIOUS SQUARES

1 cup all-purpose flour
2 tablespoons sugar
½ cup butter, softened
3 eggs
1½ cups firmly packed brown sugar
2 tablespoons all-purpose flour
1 teaspoon baking powder
1 cup chopped pecans
½ cup flaked coconut
1 teaspoon vanilla extract
Frosting (recipe follows)

Combine 1 cup flour and 2 tablespoons sugar. Using hands, blend in butter until dough is smooth. Press dough evenly into bottom of a greased 9-inch square baking dish. Bake at 325° for 10 to 15 minutes.

Combine eggs, brown sugar, 2 tablespoons flour, and baking powder in a large mixing bowl, beating well. Stir in pecans, coconut, and vanilla. Pour mixture evenly over baked crust. Bake at 325° for 20 to 25 minutes. Cool in pan. Spread with frosting, and cut into 1½-inch squares. Remove from pan carefully to avoid breaking bottom crust. Yield: 3 dozen.

Frosting:

2 tablespoons butter, melted
1½ cups sifted powdered sugar
2 tablespoons half-and-half

Combine all ingredients, beating until smooth. Additional powdered sugar may be added if necessary. Yield: frosting for 3 dozen squares.

CHINESE CHEWS

3 eggs
1 cup sugar
¾ cup all-purpose flour
1 teaspoon baking powder
¼ teaspoon salt
1 cup chopped dates
1 cup chopped pecans
Sifted powdered sugar

Beat eggs until thick and lemon colored; gradually add 1 cup sugar, beating well. Combine flour, baking powder, and salt; add to egg mixture, beating well. Fold in dates and pecans. Spread batter evenly in a greased 13- x 9- x 2-inch baking pan. Bake at 300° for 35 minutes. Cut into 3- x 1-inch bars; remove to wire racks to cool. Sprinkle with powdered sugar before serving. Yield: about 3 dozen.

DATE FILLS

2 cups all-purpose flour
¾ teaspoon baking soda
¾ teaspoon salt
¾ cup shortening, softened
¾ cup firmly packed brown sugar
⅓ cup water
2 cups quick-cooking or regular oats, uncooked
Filling (recipe follows)

Combine flour, soda, and salt in a large mixing bowl. Add shortening, sugar, and water; beat until smooth. Stir in oats.

Spread half of dough in a greased 13- x 9- x 2-inch baking pan. Spread filling evenly over dough. Roll out remaining dough between 2 sheets of waxed paper to form a 13- x 9-inch rectangle. Remove top sheet of waxed paper; place dough over filling. Remove remaining sheet of waxed paper; press dough lightly around edges to seal. Bake at 350° for 30 to 35 minutes. Cool in pan, and cut into 3- x 1½-inch bars. Yield: about 2 dozen.

Filling:

2 cups chopped pitted dates
¾ cup sugar
Grated rind of 1 orange
¼ cup orange juice
¾ cup water

Combine dates, sugar, orange rind, juice, and water in a medium saucepan. Cook over low heat until thickened, stirring frequently. Cool. Yield: filling for about 2 dozen bars.

DATE-FILLED OATMEAL BARS

2 cups all-purpose flour
2 cups quick-cooking oats, uncooked
1 teaspoon baking soda
¼ teaspoon salt
1 cup firmly packed brown sugar
¾ cup butter or margarine
1 (8-ounce) package pitted dates, chopped
1 cup sugar
1 cup water

Combine flour, oats, soda, salt, and brown sugar. Cut in butter with a pastry blender until mixture resembles coarse meal. Press half of mixture into an ungreased 12- x 8- x 2-inch baking pan.

Combine dates, 1 cup sugar, and water in a medium saucepan; cook over low heat until sugar dissolves and dates are soft. (Mixture should be thick and mushy.) Spread mixture evenly over dough in pan; cover with remaining oats mixture. Bake at 325° for 40 minutes or until lightly browned. Cut into 2- x 1-inch bars while warm. Remove to wire racks to cool. Yield: 4 dozen.

FIG-NUT SQUARES

2 eggs
½ cup sugar
½ teaspoon vanilla extract
½ cup all-purpose flour
½ teaspoon baking powder
½ teaspoon salt
1½ cups finely chopped dried figs
1 cup chopped pecans

Beat eggs in a medium mixing bowl until foamy; gradually add sugar and vanilla, beating well.

Combine flour, baking powder, and salt; add to egg mixture, stirring well. Stir in figs and pecans; spread in a greased 9-inch square baking pan. Bake at 350° for 25 to 30 minutes. Cut into 1½-inch squares, and remove to wire racks to cool. Yield: 3 dozen.

Note: 2 cups finely chopped dates may be used in place of figs.

FRUIT BARS

1 cup raisins
2 tablespoons candied orange rind
¼ cup chopped candied cherries
¼ cup finely chopped citron
½ cup chopped walnuts
½ teaspoon lemon extract
¼ cup orange juice
½ cup shortening
1 cup sugar
1 egg
2¼ cups all-purpose flour
1 teaspoon baking powder
½ teaspoon baking soda
½ teaspoon salt
½ teaspoon ground cinnamon
½ teaspoon ground nutmeg

Combine raisins with hot water to cover in a small mixing bowl. Let stand 5 minutes. Drain and dry on a paper towel; chop. Set aside.

Combine orange rind, cherries, citron, walnuts, lemon extract, and orange juice, stirring well. Set aside.

Cream shortening in a large mixing bowl; gradually add sugar, beating well. Add egg, beating well.

Combine flour, baking powder, soda, salt, cinnamon, nutmeg, and chopped raisins; blend well. Add to creamed mixture, stirring until smooth. Add reserved fruit mixture, stirring well. Cover and let dough stand 1 hour. Press dough evenly into a greased 13- x 9- x 2-inch baking pan. Bake at 400° for 12 to 15 minutes. Cut into 2- x 1-inch bars. Remove from pan immediately, and cool on wire racks. Yield: about 4½ dozen.

CANDIED FRUIT BARS

2 eggs
1 cup firmly packed brown sugar
2 teaspoons vanilla extract
1 cup all-purpose flour
1 teaspoon baking powder
½ teaspoon salt
⅔ cup chopped pecans
1 cup chopped candied fruit
½ cup seedless raisins
  Sifted powdered sugar

Beat eggs until thick and lemon colored; gradually add brown sugar and vanilla, beating well.

Combine flour, baking powder, and salt; add to egg mixture. Fold in pecans, candied fruit, and raisins. Spoon mixture into a greased and waxed paper-lined 11- x 7- x 2-inch baking pan. Bake at 350° for 30 minutes until firm and lightly browned. Remove to a wire rack to cool; remove waxed paper. Cut into 3- x 1-inch bars, and sprinkle with powdered sugar. Yield: about 2 dozen.

HOLIDAY FRUIT BARS

2 eggs
1 cup sifted powdered sugar
⅓ cup butter or margarine, melted
¾ cup sifted all-purpose flour
1½ teaspoons baking powder
¼ teaspoon salt
1 cup coarsely chopped pecans or walnuts
1 cup chopped pitted dates
¾ cup chopped candied fruit
1 cup sifted powdered sugar
2 tablespoons water

Beat eggs until thick and lemon colored in a large mixing bowl. Gradually add 1 cup sugar and butter; beat well.

Sift together flour, baking powder, and salt in a medium mixing bowl.

Spread pecans and fruit on a sheet of waxed paper; sift ½ cup flour mixture over top. Turn to coat well. Add remaining flour mixture to egg mixture, beating well. Stir in coated pecans and fruit.

Pour batter into a greased 9-inch square baking pan. Bake at 325° for 30 to 35 minutes. Cut into 2- x 1-inch bars, and remove to wire racks.

Combine 1 cup powdered sugar and water in a small mixing bowl; beat with a wire whisk until smooth. Spread a thin layer over warm bars, and cool completely. Yield: about 3 dozen.

HOLLY SQUARES

1 cup all-purpose flour
1 teaspoon baking powder
½ teaspoon salt
½ cup butter or margarine, melted
1 egg
½ cup evaporated milk
½ cup sugar
1 cup firmly packed brown sugar
1 cup regular oats, uncooked
1 cup chopped pecans or walnuts
1 cup chopped dates
¼ cup chopped candied fruit
  Glaze (recipe follows)
  Red and green candied cherries

Combine flour, baking powder, and salt in a large mixing bowl, mixing well. Add butter, egg, milk, and sugar; beat until well blended.

Combine oats, pecans, dates, and candied fruit; add to flour mixture. Spread mixture in a greased 13- x 9- x 2-inch baking pan. Bake at 350° for 45 to 50 minutes. Cool. Drizzle cookies with glaze; cut into 2-inch squares or diamonds, and arrange pieces of cherries on top of each square to resemble holly. Yield: about 2 dozen.

Glaze:

1 cup sifted powdered sugar
¼ teaspoon salt
2 tablespoons milk
½ teaspoon vanilla extract

Combine all ingredients, beating with a wire whisk until smooth. Yield: glaze for about 2 dozen squares.

RUM BARS

4½ cups chopped pecans, divided
1 cup butter or margarine,
   softened
2¼ cups firmly packed brown sugar
4 eggs
2 tablespoons vanilla extract
2¼ cups all-purpose flour
2 cups candied red cherries,
   chopped
1½ cups chopped candied pineapple
½ cup chopped candied citron
Light rum

Sprinkle 3 cups pecans evenly over a greased 15- x 10- x 1-inch jellyroll pan; set aside.

Cream butter in a large mixing bowl; gradually add sugar, beating well. Add eggs, one at a time, beating well after each addition; stir in vanilla. Gradually add flour, stirring well. Spoon batter into prepared pan.

Combine cherries, pineapple, citron, and remaining pecans in a large mixing bowl; mix well. Gently press mixture into top of batter in pan. Bake at 350° for 1 hour and 15 minutes or until lightly browned. Cool slightly; cut into 2- x 1-inch bars. Remove to wire racks to cool completely. Sprinkle rum over each bar. Yield: about 6 dozen.

Note: Rum Bars may be stored 2 to 3 weeks in airtight containers to mellow.

LEMON SQUARES

⅔ cup butter or margarine
1½ cups all-purpose flour
4 eggs
2 cups firmly packed brown sugar
1½ cups shredded coconut
¼ teaspoon baking powder
1 teaspoon vanilla extract
1⅓ cups sifted powdered sugar
2 tablespoons grated lemon rind
3 tablespoons fresh lemon juice

Cut butter into flour with a pastry blender until mixture resembles coarse meal. Press mixture evenly into an ungreased 12- x 8- x 2-inch baking pan. Bake at 350° for 20 minutes.

Beat eggs; add brown sugar, coconut, baking powder, and vanilla, mixing well. Spread over baked crust; return to oven, and bake 25 to 30 minutes.

Combine powdered sugar, lemon rind, and juice in a medium mixing bowl, beating until smooth. Spread glaze over warm cookies in pan. Cut into 2-inch squares. Leave uncovered, at least overnight, before storing in an airtight container. Yield: 2 dozen.

Note: Lemon Squares may be cut into larger squares and topped with vanilla ice cream.

DELICATE LEMON SQUARES

1 cup all-purpose flour
¼ cup sifted powdered
   sugar
½ cup butter or margarine
2 eggs, beaten
1 cup sugar
½ teaspoon grated lemon
   rind
3 tablespoons lemon juice
2 tablespoons all-purpose flour
½ teaspoon baking
   powder
2 tablespoons sifted powdered
   sugar

Combine 1 cup flour and ¼ cup powdered sugar; cut in butter with a pastry blender until mixture resembles coarse meal. Press mixture evenly into a 9-inch square baking pan. Bake at 350° for 15 minutes.

Combine eggs, 1 cup sugar, lemon rind, and juice in a medium mixing bowl; beat well. Combine 2 tablespoons flour and baking powder. Add to egg mixture, stirring well. Pour mixture over baked crust. Bake at 350° for 20 minutes or until lightly browned and set. Sprinkle lightly with 2 tablespoons powdered sugar. Let cool, and cut into 1½-inch squares. Store in airtight containers. Yield: 3 dozen.

LEMON CRUMB SQUARES

1 (15-ounce) can sweetened
   condensed milk
1 teaspoon grated lemon rind
½ cup fresh lemon juice
⅔ cup butter or margarine
1 cup firmly packed dark brown
   sugar
1½ cups all-purpose flour
1 teaspoon baking powder
½ teaspoon salt
1 cup regular or quick-cooking
   oats, uncooked

Combine milk, lemon rind, and juice; set aside.

Cream butter in a large mixing bowl; gradually add sugar, beating until light and fluffy. Combine flour, baking powder, salt, and oats. Add to creamed mixture; blend until mixture resembles coarse meal.

Press half of oats mixture firmly into a greased 12- x 8- x 2-inch baking pan. Spread reserved milk mixture evenly over top. Cover with remaining oats mixture. Bake at 350° for 25 minutes or until edges are browned. Cool in pan 15 minutes; cut into 2-inch squares. Chill in pan until firm. Yield: 2 dozen.

LEMON CURD BARS

1 cup all-purpose flour
1 teaspoon baking powder
½ cup butter or margarine
1 egg, lightly beaten
4 egg yolks, lightly
   beaten
1 cup sugar
   Grated rind of 2 lemons
   Juice of 2 lemons
   Topping (recipe follows)

Combine flour and baking powder in a large mixing bowl. Cut in butter with a pastry blender until mixture resembles coarse meal; add 1 egg, and mix well. Press mixture evenly into a lightly greased 9-inch square baking pan. Set aside.

Combine egg yolks, sugar, lemon rind, and juice in top of a double boiler. Cook over medium heat until thickened and smooth, stirring constantly to prevent lumping. Cool mixture, and spread over crust in pan. Spread topping evenly over lemon mixture. Bake at 350° for 20 to 30 minutes. Cut into 3- x 1½-inch bars. Yield: 1½ dozen.

Topping:

1 egg, well beaten
¾ cup sugar
1 cup flaked coconut

Combine egg and sugar in a small mixing bowl, beating until light and fluffy. Stir in coconut, mixing gently until blended. Yield: topping for 1½ dozen bars.

LIME SQUARES

1 cup all-purpose flour
¼ cup butter, softened
½ cup chopped pecans
¼ cup sugar
2 eggs
2 tablespoons lime juice
1 to 1½ tablespoons grated lime
   rind
1 cup sugar
2 tablespoons all-purpose flour
½ teaspoon baking powder
   Powdered sugar (optional)

Combine 1 cup flour, butter, pecans, and ¼ cup sugar; mix until crumbly, using a pastry blender. Press into a greased and floured 12- x 8-inch baking pan. Bake at 350° for 15 minutes.

Beat eggs with a fork, adding lime juice, rind, 1 cup sugar, 2 tablespoons flour, and baking powder. Pour mixture over crust. Bake an additional 25 minutes. Cool. Sprinkle with powdered sugar, if desired. Yield: about 3½ dozen.

ORANGE SLICE SQUARES

½ cup butter or margarine, melted
2 cups firmly packed brown
   sugar
4 eggs, beaten
2 cups all purpose flour
1 pound candied orange slices,
   finely chopped
1 cup chopped pecans
1 cup sifted powdered sugar

Combine butter and brown sugar in a large mixing bowl; stir in eggs, mixing well. Add flour, candied orange slices, and pecans; stir until blended.

Spread batter into a well-greased 15- x 10- x 1-inch jellyroll pan. Bake at 350° for 25 minutes. Cool 15 minutes in pan. Cut into 2-inch squares; cut squares in half diagonally, if desired. Cool completely in pan. Remove from pan, and sprinkle all sides with powdered sugar. Yield: about 3 dozen.

MARMALADE MERINGUE BARS

¼ cup plus 2 tablespoons butter or
   margarine, softened
½ cup sugar, divided
2 eggs, separated
1 teaspoon grated orange
   rind
1 teaspoon vanilla extract
1 cup all-purpose flour
½ cup wheat germ, toasted and
   divided
½ cup finely chopped pecans,
   divided
¼ teaspoon salt
⅓ cup orange marmalade
   Sifted powdered sugar

Cream butter in a medium mixing bowl; gradually add ¼ cup sugar, beating until light and fluffy. Add egg yolks, orange rind, and vanilla, beating until well blended.

Combine flour, ¼ cup wheat germ, ¼ cup pecans, and salt; add to creamed mixture, mixing well. Press dough evenly into an ungreased 8-inch square baking pan, making a 1-inch side crust. Bake at 350° for 12 to 15 minutes or until golden brown.

Beat egg whites (at room temperature) until soft peaks form; gradually add remaining ¼ cup sugar, 1 tablespoon at a time, beating until stiff peaks form. Fold in remaining ¼ cup wheat germ and ¼ cup pecans; set aside.

Spread marmalade over warm crust; top with meringue mixture. Bake at 350° for 18 to 20 minutes or until golden brown. Cool in pan on a wire rack; sprinkle with powdered sugar; cut into 4- x 1-inch bars. Store in an airtight container up to 1 week. Yield: about 1½ dozen.

GLAZED SPICE BARS

¾ cup vegetable oil
¼ cup honey
1 cup sugar
1 egg
2 cups all-purpose flour
1 teaspoon baking soda
½ teaspoon salt
1 teaspoon ground cinnamon
1 cup chopped walnuts
   Glaze (recipe follows)

Combine all ingredients, except glaze, in a large mixing bowl; mix until well blended. Press dough evenly into an ungreased 13- x 9- x 2-inch baking pan. Bake at 350° for 25 to 30 minutes. Cool completely on a wire rack; drizzle glaze over top. Let glaze set before cutting into 3- x 1-inch bars. Yield: about 3 dozen.

Glaze:

½ cup sifted powdered
   sugar
½ teaspoon vanilla extract
1 teaspoon water
1½ teaspoons mayonnaise

Combine all ingredients; beat with a wire whisk until mixture is smooth. Yield: glaze for about 3 dozen bars.

PEANUT BUTTER FINGERS

1   cup all-purpose flour
½   cup sugar
½   cup firmly packed brown sugar
½   teaspoon baking soda
¼   teaspoon salt
½   cup butter or margarine,
      softened
⅓   cup crunchy peanut butter
1   egg
1   cup regular oats, uncooked
1   (12-ounce) package semisweet
      chocolate morsels
½   cup sifted powdered sugar
¼   cup crunchy peanut butter
2   to 4 tablespoons milk

Combine first 9 ingredients in a large mixing bowl; mix well.

Press dough into a greased 13- x 9- x 2-inch baking pan. Bake at 350° for 20 minutes. Remove from oven, and sprinkle with chocolate morsels. Let stand 5 minutes or until morsels melt; spread evenly over surface.

Combine powdered sugar, ¼ cup peanut butter, and milk in a small mixing bowl; beat well. Drizzle mixture over cookies. Cut into 2- x 1-inch bars. Yield: about 4½ dozen.

PUMPKIN BARS

1   (3½-ounce) can flaked coconut
1   cup graham cracker crumbs
1   cup chopped walnuts
¼   cup butter or margarine, melted
2   cups cooked, mashed pumpkin
1   (14-ounce) can sweetened
      condensed milk
2   eggs
2   tablespoons pumpkin pie spice
½   teaspoon salt

Combine coconut, graham cracker crumbs, walnuts, and melted butter in a large mixing bowl; mix well. Press two-thirds of mixture into an ungreased 13- x 9- x 2-inch baking pan.

Combine pumpkin, milk, eggs, spice, and salt. Spoon over coconut mixture; sprinkle remaining coconut mixture over top. Bake at 375° for 30 to 35 minutes. Cool in pan; chill thoroughly. Cut into 3- x 2-inch bars. Yield: about 2 dozen.

ZUCCHINI BARS

1½   cups firmly packed brown
        sugar
½   cup butter or margarine,
        softened
¼   cup vegetable oil
2   eggs
2   tablespoons water
1   teaspoon vanilla extract
¼   teaspoon ground nutmeg
1½   cups shreds of wheat bran
        cereal
1½   cups all-purpose flour
½   cup whole wheat flour
1   teaspoon baking soda
½   teaspoon salt
2½   cups grated zucchini
1   cup raisins
1   cup flaked coconut

Combine sugar, butter, and oil in a large mixing bowl; beat until light and fluffy. Add eggs, water, vanilla, and nutmeg; mix well.

Combine cereal, flour, soda, and salt; add to creamed mixture alternately with zucchini. Stir in raisins and coconut. Spread in a greased 13- x 9- x 2-inch baking pan. Bake at 360° for 40 minutes. Cool; cut into 3- x 1½-inch bars. Yield: about 2 dozen.

LONDON BARS

¾   cup butter or margarine,
        softened
1¼   cups sugar, divided
4   eggs, separated
2¼   cups all-purpose flour
1   (12-ounce) jar raspberry
        preserves
1   teaspoon vanilla extract
½   cup chopped pecans

Cream butter in a large mixing bowl; gradually add ¼ cup sugar, beating until light and fluffy. Add egg yolks, one at a time, beating well after each addition. Stir in flour, blending well.

Press mixture into a lightly greased 15- x 10- x 1-inch jellyroll pan. Bake at 350° for 25 minutes or until lightly browned. Remove from oven; cool in pan. Spread raspberry preserves over baked crust.

Beat egg whites (at room temperature) in a medium mixing bowl until foamy. Gradually add remaining sugar, 1 tablespoon at a time, beating until stiff peaks form. Fold in vanilla. Spread meringue over preserves. Sprinkle with pecans. Bake at 350° for 15 minutes or until lightly browned. Cool slightly; cut into 2- x 1-inch bars with a warm knife. Remove to wire racks to cool completely. Store in airtight containers. Yield: about 6 dozen.

RASPBERRY JAM LOGS

1 cup all-purpose flour
1 teaspoon baking powder
½ cup butter or margarine, melted and slightly cooled
1 egg, beaten
1 teaspoon milk
⅓ cup raspberry jam
¼ cup butter or margarine, softened
1 cup sugar
1 egg, beaten
1 teaspoon vanilla extract
1 (7-ounce) can flaked coconut

Combine flour, baking powder, and ½ cup butter in a medium mixing bowl, mixing well; stir in 1 egg and milk.

Press mixture into a greased 12- x 8- x 2-inch baking dish. Spread jam over mixture; set aside.

Cream ¼ cup butter in a large mixing bowl; gradually add sugar, beating well. Stir in remaining egg and vanilla, mixing well. Add coconut, and stir well; spread mixture over jam. Bake at 350° for 30 minutes. Cool and cut into 3- x 1½-inch bars. Yield: about 1½ dozen.

SEVEN-LAYER SQUARES

¼ cup plus 1 tablespoon butter or margarine
1½ cups graham cracker crumbs
1 cup flaked coconut
1 cup semisweet chocolate morsels
1 cup butterscotch morsels
1 cup chopped pecans
1 (15-ounce) can sweetened condensed milk

Place butter in a 9-inch square baking pan, and bake at 325° until melted; remove from oven. Layer graham cracker crumbs, coconut, chocolate morsels, butterscotch morsels, and pecans in pan with melted butter. (Do not stir.) Spread condensed milk evenly over top. Bake at 325° for 30 minutes. Cut into 1½-inch squares, and remove to wire racks to cool. Yield: 3 dozen.

Note: Walnuts may be substituted for pecans. This recipe freezes well.

DROP COOKIES

PECAN KISS CAKES

4 egg whites
1½ cups sugar
1 teaspoon vanilla extract
1 cup chopped pecans

Beat egg whites (at room temperature) in a medium mixing bowl until foamy; add sugar, 2 tablespoons at a time, beating until stiff peaks form. Fold in vanilla and pecans.

Drop mixture by heaping teaspoonfuls 2 inches apart onto waxed paper-lined cookie sheets. Bake at 250° for 55 minutes. Remove from waxed paper, and cool on wire racks. Store immediately in airtight containers. Yield: about 8 dozen.

PRALINE KISSES

1 egg white
1 cup firmly packed brown
    sugar
1 teaspoon vanilla extract
1½ cups finely chopped
    pecans

Beat egg white (at room temperature) until foamy. Gradually add sugar, 2 tablespoons at a time, beating until stiff peaks form and sugar dissolves. Fold in vanilla and pecans.

Drop mixture by heaping tablespoonfuls 3 inches apart onto ungreased cookie sheets. Bake at 225° for 1½

hours. Turn oven off; cool cookies in oven at least 1 hour. (Do not open oven door.) Remove from cookie sheets, using a spatula. Serve immediately, or store in airtight containers. Yield: about 3½ dozen.

ORANGE-FILLED KISSES

4 egg whites
1 cup sifted powdered sugar
   Orange Filling

Beat egg whites (at room temperature) until foamy; gradually add sugar, beating constantly until stiff peaks form.

Drop mixture by teaspoonfuls 2 inches apart onto aluminum foil-lined cookie sheets. Bake at 250° for 1 hour. Cool; remove from aluminum foil. Spread Orange Filling on bottom sides of half the cookies. Top with remaining cookies to form sandwiches. Yield: 2 dozen.

Orange Filling:

2 tablespoons butter or margarine,
    softened
1 cup sifted powdered sugar
2 teaspoons milk
1 teaspoon grated orange rind
   Orange food coloring

Cream butter; gradually add sugar, beating well. Add milk and orange rind, stirring well. Tint with orange food coloring. Yield: filling for 2 dozen cookies.

BREADCRUMB MERINGUES

4 egg whites
Dash of salt
2 cups sugar
1 cup fine dry breadcrumbs
1 cup finely chopped pecans
1 teaspoon vanilla extract

Beat egg whites (at room temperature) in a medium mixing bowl until foamy; add salt. Gradually add sugar, 2 tablespoons at a time, beating until stiff peaks form. Fold in breadcrumbs, pecans, and vanilla.

Drop mixture by heaping teaspoonfuls 2 inches apart onto waxed paper-lined cookie sheets. Bake at 350° for 15 minutes. Remove from waxed paper, and cool on wire racks. Yield: 7 dozen.

CHOCOLATE CHIP FORGOTTEN COOKIES

2 egg whites
Dash of salt
⅔ cup sugar
½ teaspoon vanilla extract
1 (6-ounce) package semisweet chocolate morsels
1 cup chopped pecans

Preheat oven to 350°. Beat egg whites (at room temperature) in a large mixing bowl until foamy; add salt. Gradually add sugar, 2 tablespoons at a time, beating until stiff peaks form. Fold in vanilla, chocolate morsels, and pecans.

Drop mixture by heaping teaspoonfuls 2 inches apart onto aluminum foil-lined cookie sheets. Place in oven, and immediately turn off heat. Do not open oven door for at least 12 hours. Gently remove cookies from aluminum foil, and cool on wire racks. Store in airtight containers. Yield: about 3 dozen.

PEPPERMINT MERINGUES

2 egg whites
½ teaspoon peppermint extract
½ cup sugar
6 drops red food coloring (optional)
1 (6-ounce) package semisweet chocolate morsels

Combine egg whites (at room temperature) and peppermint extract; beat until foamy. Gradually add sugar, 2 tablespoons at a time, beating until stiff peaks form. (Do not underbeat.) Fold in food coloring, if desired, and chocolate morsels.

Drop mixture by rounded teaspoonfuls 2 inches apart onto greased cookie sheets. Bake at 200° for 1 hour or until dry and set. (Cookies should not brown.) Remove to wire racks to cool. Yield: about 2½ dozen.

CHOCOLATE-PECAN MERINGUES

2 egg whites
⅛ teaspoon salt
⅛ teaspoon cream of tartar
¾ cup sugar
1 (6-ounce) package semisweet chocolate morsels
⅔ cup chopped pecans
1 teaspoon vanilla extract

Beat egg whites (at room temperature), salt, and cream of tarter until foamy; gradually add sugar, beating until stiff peaks form. Fold in chocolate, pecans, and vanilla.

Drop mixture by heaping teaspoonfuls 2 inches apart onto parchment-lined cookie sheets. Bake at 300° for 25 minutes. Remove from parchment, using a sharp spatula, and cool on wire racks. Store in airtight containers. Yield: 3 dozen.

CHOCOLATE-WALNUT MERINGUES

1 (6-ounce) package semisweet
    chocolate morsels
2 egg whites
½ cup sugar
½ teaspoon vinegar
⅛ teaspoon salt
½ teaspoon vanilla extract
¾ cup chopped walnuts

Melt chocolate morsels in top of a double boiler over simmering water. Let cool slightly.

Beat egg whites (at room temperature) until foamy; gradually add sugar, 2 tablespoons at a time, beating until stiff peaks form. Add vinegar, salt, and vanilla, beating well. Fold in melted chocolate and walnuts.

Drop mixture by teaspoonfuls 2 inches apart onto well-greased cookie sheets. Bake at 300° for 20 minutes. Remove from cookie sheets, and cool on wire racks. Store in airtight containers. Yield: about 3 dozen.

COCONUT PUFFS

3 egg whites
¼ teaspoon salt
¼ teaspoon cream of tartar
1 cup sugar
½ teaspoon almond
    extract
1 cup flaked coconut
1 cup regular or quick-cooking
    oats, uncooked
½ cup chopped pecans

Beat egg whites (at room temperature), salt, and cream of tartar until foamy. Gradually add sugar and almond extract, beating until stiff peaks form. Fold in coconut, oats, and pecans.

Drop mixture by teaspoonfuls onto greased cookie sheets. Bake at 325° for 20 minutes. Cool slightly on cookie sheets. Remove to wire racks to cool completely. Yield: about 4 dozen.

MERINGUE FRUIT DROPS

3 egg whites
1 cup sugar
½ teaspoon salt
1 cup flaked coconut
1 cup chopped pecans or walnuts
1 cup chopped dates
1 teaspoon vanilla extract
½ teaspoon almond extract

Beat egg whites (at room temperature) until foamy. Gradually add sugar, 2 tablespoons at a time, beating until stiff peaks form. Fold in pecans, dates, and flavorings.

Drop mixture by teaspoonfuls 2 inches apart onto greased cookie sheets. Bake at 325° for 20 minutes. (Do not overbake.) Remove to wire racks to cool. Store in airtight containers. Yield: about 3 dozen.

COCONUT MACAROONS

2 egg whites
    Dash of salt
½ cup sugar
½ teaspoon vanilla extract
1 cup flaked coconut
½ cup chopped pecans (optional)

Beat egg whites (at room temperature) and salt in a medium mixing bowl until foamy. Add sugar and vanilla, beating until stiff peaks form. Fold in coconut and pecans, if desired.

Drop mixture by teaspoonfuls 2 inches apart onto parchment-lined cookie sheets. Bake at 350° for 15 to 20 minutes. Remove from oven, and place cookie sheets on a damp cloth for a few seconds. Remove macaroons to wire racks to cool. Yield: 2½ dozen.

DATE-NUT MACAROONS

1 (8-ounce) package chopped
    dates
1 cup chopped pecans
1 cup sifted powdered sugar,
    divided
2 egg whites
½ teaspoon vanilla extract

Combine dates, pecans, and ½ cup sugar in a small mixing bowl. Set aside.

Beat egg whites (at room temperature) until soft peaks form. Add remaining sugar, 2 tablespoons at a time, beating until stiff peaks form. Fold in reserved date mixture and vanilla.

Drop mixture by heaping teaspoonfuls 2 inches apart onto greased cookie sheets. Bake at 200° for 1 hour. Cool slightly on cookie sheets, and remove to wire racks. Yield: about 5 dozen.

STIR-'N-DROP SUGAR COOKIES

2 eggs, beaten
⅔ cup vegetable oil
2 teaspoons vanilla
    extract
1 teaspoon grated lemon
    rind
¾ cup sugar
2 cups all-purpose flour
2 teaspoons baking
    powder
½ teaspoon salt

Combine eggs, oil, vanilla, and lemon rind in a large mixing bowl; add sugar, stirring until well blended.

Combine flour, baking powder, and salt in a medium mixing bowl; add to egg mixture, stirring well.

Drop dough by teaspoonfuls 2 inches apart onto ungreased cookie sheets. Flatten cookies with greased bottom of a glass dipped in sugar. Bake at 400° for 8 to 10 minutes or until lightly browned. Remove immediately from cookie sheets, and cool on wire racks. Store in airtight containers. Yield: about 3 dozen.

OLD-FASHIONED SUGAR COOKIES

1 cup shortening
2 cups sugar, divided
2 eggs
1 teaspoon lemon extract
1 teaspoon vanilla extract
2½ cups all-purpose flour
2 teaspoons baking powder
¼ teaspoon salt

Cream shortening; add 1½ cups sugar, beating until light and fluffy. Add eggs and flavorings; beat well.

Combine flour, baking powder, and salt. Add to creamed mixture; mix.

Drop dough by heaping teaspoonfuls 3 inches apart onto greased cookie sheets. Press cookies with a fork to flatten. Sprinkle cookies with remaining sugar. Bake at 375° for 10 minutes or until lightly browned. Remove to wire racks to cool. Yield: 8 dozen.

BUTTERSCOTCH DROPS

¼ cup butter or margarine,
    softened
1¼ cups firmly packed brown
    sugar
1 egg
⅔ cup all-purpose flour
1 teaspoon baking powder
¼ teaspoon salt
½ teaspoon vanilla
    extract
½ cup chopped pecans
¾ cup golden raisins, washed,
    drained, and coarsely chopped

Cream butter; gradually add sugar, beating well. Add egg; beat well.

Combine flour, baking powder, and salt; add to creamed mixture, blending well. Stir in vanilla, pecans, and raisins. Drop by teaspoonfuls 2 inches apart onto greased cookie sheets. Bake at 325° for 15 minutes. Cool slightly on cookie sheets; remove to wire racks to cool completely. Yield: 3½ dozen.

BUTTERSCOTCH COOKIES

¾ cup butter or margarine,
    softened
1 cup sugar
2 eggs
1½ cups all-purpose flour
¾ teaspoon baking soda
1 teaspoon salt
1 teaspoon ground cinnamon
⅓ cup milk
1½ cups quick-cooking or regular
    oats, uncooked
1 (6-ounce) package butterscotch
    morsels
1 cup raisins
½ cup chopped pecans (optional)

Cream butter in a large mixing bowl; gradually add sugar, beating until light and fluffy. Add eggs, beating well.

Combine flour, soda, salt, and cinnamon; add to creamed mixture alternately with milk, beginning and ending with flour mixture. Stir in remaining ingredients, blending well.

Drop dough by tablespoonfuls 2 inches apart onto greased cookie sheets. Bake at 350° for 12 to 14 minutes. Remove to wire racks to cool. Yield: 4 dozen.

BROWNIE DROP COOKIES

2 (4-ounce) packages sweet baking
    chocolate
1 tablespoon butter or margarine
2 eggs
¾ cup sugar
¼ cup all-purpose flour
¼ teaspoon baking powder
⅛ teaspoon salt
½ teaspoon vanilla extract
¾ cup chopped pecans

Melt chocolate and butter in top of a double boiler over simmering water.

Beat eggs until foamy; gradually add sugar, beating 5 minutes or until thickened. Add chocolate mixture; beat well.

Combine flour, baking powder, and salt in a medium mixing bowl. Add to egg mixture, stirring until well blended. Fold in vanilla and pecans.

Drop dough by teaspoonfuls 2 inches apart onto greased cookies sheets. Bake at 350° for 10 minutes or until set. Cool slightly on cookie sheets; remove to wire racks. Yield: about 4 dozen.

CHOCOLATE TWINKLES

½ cup shortening
1 cup sugar
2 eggs, beaten
3 (1-ounce) squares unsweetened
    chocolate, melted
1 teaspoon vanilla extract
2 cups all-purpose flour
2 teaspoons baking powder
¼ teaspoon salt
½ cup milk
¾ cup chopped black walnuts
    Walnut halves

Cream shortening; add sugar, beating well. Add eggs and melted chocolate, beating well. Stir in vanilla.

Combine flour, baking powder, and salt in a medium mixing bowl. Add to creamed mixture alternately with milk, beginning and ending with flour mixture. Stir in chopped black walnuts.

Drop dough by teaspoonfuls 2 inches apart onto greased cookie sheets. Gently press a walnut half in center of each cookie. Bake at 350° for 10 to 12 minutes. Cool on wire racks. Yield: 4 dozen.

TIGER COOKIES

¾ cup butter or margarine,
    softened
1 cup sugar
2 eggs
1 teaspoon vanilla extract
2 cups all-purpose flour
1 teaspoon baking soda
½ teaspoon salt
3 cups sugar-frosted corn flake
    cereal, crushed
1 (6-ounce) package semisweet
    chocolate morsels

Cream butter in a large mixing bowl; gradually add sugar, beating until light and fluffy. Add eggs, beating well. Stir in vanilla.

Combine flour, soda, and salt; add to creamed mixture, mixing well. Stir in crushed cereal.

Melt chocolate in top of a double boiler over simmering water. Swirl melted chocolate lightly through dough, leaving streaks of chocolate.

Drop dough by heaping teaspoonfuls 2 inches apart onto ungreased cookie sheets. Bake at 375° for 10 to 12 minutes. Remove to wire racks to cool. Yield: 5 dozen.

DOUBLE TREAT COOKIES

½ cup butter, margarine, or
  shortening, softened
½ cup crunchy peanut butter
½ cup firmly packed brown
  sugar
½ cup sugar
1 egg
½ teaspoon vanilla extract
1¼ cups all-purpose
  flour
1 teaspoon baking soda
¼ teaspoon salt
1 (6-ounce) package semisweet
  chocolate morsels

Cream butter and peanut butter in a large mixing bowl; gradually add sugar, beating until light and fluffy. Add egg, beating until well blended. Stir in vanilla, blending well.

Combine flour, soda, and salt in a medium mixing bowl; add to creamed mixture, mixing until well blended. Stir in chocolate morsels.

Drop dough by rounded teaspoonfuls 2 inches apart onto ungreased cookie sheets. Bake at 350° for 8 to 10 minutes. Remove to wire racks to cool. Store in airtight containers. Yield: about 4½ dozen.

Note: Butterscotch morsels may be substituted for the chocolate morsels, if desired.

SOUR CREAM CHOCOLATE DROPS

2 (1-ounce) squares unsweetened
  chocolate
½ cup shortening, softened
1½ cups sugar
2 eggs
1 (8-ounce) carton commercial
  sour cream
1 teaspoon vanilla extract
2¾ cups all-purpose flour
½ teaspoon baking
  powder
½ teaspoon baking soda
½ teaspoon salt
1 cup corn flakes
Frosting (recipe follows)

Melt chocolate in top of a double boiler over simmering water. Remove from heat, and set aside.

Cream shortening in a large mixing bowl; gradually add sugar, beating well. Add eggs, one at a time, beating well after each addition. Stir in sour cream and vanilla.

Combine flour, baking powder, soda, and salt in a medium mixing bowl. Stir in corn flakes, and add to creamed mixture; mix just until blended. Stir in reserved chocolate. Chill 1 hour.

Drop dough by teaspoonfuls 2 inches apart onto lightly greased cookie sheets. Bake at 425° for 8 to 10 minutes. Remove to wire racks to cool. Spread frosting evenly over each cookie. Yield: about 6 dozen.

Frosting:

1 (1-ounce) square unsweetened
  chocolate
1 tablespoon butter or margarine
3 tablespoons milk
1½ cups sifted powdered
  sugar

Melt chocolate and butter in top of a double boiler over simmering water. Add milk and powdered sugar; beat with a wire whisk until smooth. Yield: frosting for about 6 dozen cookies.

CHOCOLATE CREAM COOKIES

½ cup butter or margarine,
   softened
½ cup shortening
1 (3-ounce) package cream cheese,
   softened
1½ cups sugar
1 egg
2 tablespoons milk
½ teaspoon vanilla extract
2 (1-ounce) squares unsweetened
   chocolate, melted
2¼ cups all-purpose flour
1½ teaspoons baking powder
½ teaspoon salt
½ cup chopped pecans

Cream butter, shortening, and cream cheese; gradually add sugar, beating until light and fluffy. Add egg, milk, and vanilla; beat well. Stir in chocolate.

Sift together flour, baking powder, and salt; gradually add to creamed mixture, mixing well. Stir in pecans.

Drop dough by teaspoonfuls 2 inches apart onto greased cookie sheets. Bake at 350° for 8 to 10 minutes. Cool slightly on cookie sheets; remove to wire racks to cool completely. Yield: about 6 dozen.

HERMITS

½ cup firmly packed brown sugar
1 egg, beaten
½ teaspoon lemon extract
¼ teaspoon vanilla extract
½ cup raisins
1¼ cups bread flour
¼ teaspoon salt
½ teaspoon ground cinnamon
½ teaspoon ground allspice
¼ teaspoon ground nutmeg
¼ teaspoon ground cloves
½ cup shortening, melted
   Additional raisins

Combine sugar and egg, beating well. Stir in flavorings and ½ cup raisins.

Sift together flour, salt, and spices; add to sugar mixture, stirring well. Stir in shortening.

Drop dough by teaspoonfuls 2 inches apart onto lightly greased cookie sheets; press a raisin in center of each cookie. Bake at 350° for 8 to 10 minutes. Remove to wire racks to cool. Yield: about 3½ dozen.

PECAN HERMITS

¾ cup shortening
1½ cups firmly packed brown
   sugar
1 teaspoon ground cinnamon
½ teaspoon ground nutmeg
¼ teaspoon ground cloves
2 eggs, beaten
1 tablespoon milk
2½ cups all-purpose flour
½ teaspoon baking soda
¼ teaspoon salt
1 cup raisins, chopped
½ cup chopped pecans

Combine shortening, sugar, and spices, beating well. Add eggs and milk; beat until well blended.

Sift together flour, soda, and salt in a medium mixing bowl. Add to creamed mixture, stirring well. Fold in raisins and pecans.

Drop dough by heaping teaspoonfuls 2 inches apart onto greased cookie sheets; flatten each cookie slightly, using the back of a spoon. Bake at 350° for 12 minutes. Remove to wire racks to cool. Store in airtight containers. Yield: 5 dozen.

ROCK COOKIES

1 cup butter or margarine,
   softened
1½ cups firmly packed brown sugar
3 eggs
3 tablespoons strong brewed coffee
2½ cups all-purpose flour
1 teaspoon baking soda
1 tablespoon ground cinnamon
1 tablespoon ground allspice
1 cup raisins
1 cup chopped pecans

Cream butter; gradually add sugar, beating until light and fluffy. Add eggs; beat well. Stir in coffee.

Combine flour, soda, cinnamon, and allspice in a medium mixing bowl. Stir in raisins and pecans to coat well; add to creamed mixture.

Drop dough by heaping teaspoonfuls 2 inches apart onto greased cookie sheets. Bake at 350° for 8 minutes. Remove to wire racks to cool. Yield: about 5½ dozen.

SOUR CREAM ROCKS

½ teaspoon baking soda
⅓ cup commercial sour cream
¾ cup butter or margarine, softened
1¼ cups firmly packed brown sugar
3 eggs
2 cups all-purpose flour
1 teaspoon ground cinnamon
½ teaspoon ground nutmeg
1 cup raisins
1 cup pecan halves

Dissolve soda in sour cream; stir well. Set aside.

Cream butter in a large mixing bowl. Gradually add sugar, beating until light and fluffy. Add eggs, one at a time, beating well after each addition.

Combine flour, cinnamon, and nutmeg in a medium mixing bowl; stir in raisins and pecans to coat well. Add to creamed mixture, stirring until blended. Stir in sour cream mixture.

Drop dough by teaspoonfuls 2 inches apart onto greased cookie sheets. Bake at 375° for 8 to 10 minutes. Remove to wire racks to cool. Store in airtight containers. Yield: 8 dozen.

CHOCOLATE ROCKS

¾ cup butter or margarine, softened
2 cups firmly packed brown sugar
2 eggs
4 (1-ounce) squares unsweetened chocolate, melted
2 teaspoons vanilla extract
2 cups all-purpose flour
2 teaspoons baking powder
1 teaspoon ground cinnamon
1 cup raisins
1 cup chopped pecans

Cream butter; gradually add sugar, beating well. Add eggs; beat well. Add melted chocolate and vanilla; beat well.

Sift together flour, baking powder, and cinnamon; stir in raisins and pecans. Add to creamed mixture.

Drop dough by teaspoonfuls 2 inches apart onto greased cookie sheets. Bake at 375° for 8 to 10 minutes. Remove to wire racks to cool. Yield: 11 dozen.

CRISP MOLASSES COOKIES

½ cup plus 2 tablespoons butter or margarine, melted
1 cup sugar
½ cup molasses
2 eggs
½ teaspoon vanilla extract
1¾ cups all-purpose flour
¼ teaspoon baking soda
¼ teaspoon salt
¼ teaspoon ground mace
2 cups chopped pecans

Combine butter, sugar, and molasses in a large mixing bowl, mixing well; add eggs and vanilla, beating well.

Sift together flour, soda, salt, and mace in a medium mixing bowl; add to butter mixture, ½ cup at a time, mixing well after each addition. Stir in pecans.

Drop dough by heaping teaspoonfuls 2 inches apart onto greased and floured cookie sheets. Bake at 350° for 8 minutes. Remove to wire racks to cool. Yield: about 5 dozen.

HONEY DROPS

¾ cup butter or margarine
1 cup sugar
1 egg, separated
1 teaspoon grated orange
   rind
¼ cup honey
2 cups all-purpose flour
2 teaspoons baking
   powder
½ teaspoon salt
½ teaspoon ground mace
   Tinted flaked coconut

Cream butter in a large mixing bowl; gradually add sugar, beating until light and fluffy. Add egg yolk and orange rind; beat well. Stir in honey.

Combine flour, baking powder, salt, and mace. Gradually add to creamed mixture, blending well.

Drop dough by teaspoonfuls 2 inches apart onto ungreased cookie sheets; flatten each with a fork. Brush lightly beaten egg white over cookies; sprinkle coconut over egg white. Bake at 350° for 10 to 14 minutes. Remove to wire racks to cool. Store in airtight containers. Yield: 5 dozen.

Note: To tint coconut, sprinkle a few drops of food coloring over coconut; toss with a fork until evenly tinted.

HONEY-OATMEAL COOKIES

1 cup butter or margarine,
   softened
1 cup sugar
¼ cup honey
2 eggs
½ cup commercial sour
   cream
2 cups all-purpose flour
1 teaspoon baking soda
1 teaspoon salt
1 teaspoon ground cinnamon
1 teaspoon ground ginger
3 cups quick-cooking oats,
   uncooked
1 cup chopped dates

Cream butter; gradually add sugar and honey, beating until light and fluffy. Add eggs; beat well. Stir in sour cream, blending well.

Combine flour, soda, salt, cinnamon, and ginger in a medium mixing bowl; add to creamed mixture. Stir in oats and dates, mixing well.

Drop dough by teaspoonfuls 2 inches apart onto greased cookies sheets. Bake at 375° for 10 to 12 minutes. Cool 5 minutes on cookies sheets before removing to wire racks to cool completely. Store in airtight containers. Yield: about 8 dozen.

OATMEAL LACE COOKIES

½ cup sugar
1 egg, beaten
1½ teaspoons butter or margarine,
   melted
1¼ cups regular oats,
   uncooked
1¼ teaspoons baking powder
¼ teaspoon salt
½ teaspoon ground
   nutmeg
½ teaspoon vanilla extract

Gradually add sugar to egg in a medium mixing bowl, beating until blended. Add melted butter; mix until well blended.

Combine oats, baking powder, salt, and nutmeg; add to egg mixure, beating well. Stir in vanilla.

Drop dough by teaspoonfuls 2 inches apart onto lightly greased cookie sheets. Bake at 350° for 6 minutes or until lightly browned. Remove to wire racks to cool. Store in airtight containers. Yield: about 4 dozen.

OATMEAL-RAISIN COOKIES

½ cup butter
1 cup regular oats, uncooked
¼ cup milk
1 egg, beaten
1 cup all-purpose flour
½ cup sugar
½ teaspoon baking powder
½ teaspoon baking soda
¼ teaspoon salt
1 teaspoon ground cinnamon
1 teaspoon ground nutmeg
½ cup raisins
½ cup chopped pecans
1½ teaspoons vanilla extract

Melt butter in top of a double boiler over simmering water; add oats and milk, stirring well. Cover and cook over low heat 15 minutes. Remove from heat, and cool slightly; stir in egg.

Sift together flour, sugar, baking powder, soda, salt, cinnamon, and nutmeg; add to oats mixture, stirring well. Stir in raisins, pecans, and vanilla.

Drop dough by heaping teaspoonfuls 2 inches apart onto greased cookie sheets. Bake at 350° for 15 minutes. Cool slightly on cookie sheets. Remove to wire racks. Yield: 3½ dozen.

AMBROSIA COOKIES

1 cup butter or margarine
1 cup sugar
1 cup firmly packed brown
    sugar
2 eggs, well beaten
1 teaspoon vanilla extract
2 cups all-purpose flour
1 teaspoon baking powder
½ teaspoon baking soda
¼ teaspoon salt
1 cup flaked coconut
1½ cups quick-cooking or regular
    oats, uncooked
1 cup chopped pecans
2 cups raisins or chopped dates
1 tablespoon grated lemon rind
1 teaspoon grated orange rind

Cream butter in a large mixing bowl; gradually add sugar, beating well. Add eggs, beating well; stir in vanilla.

Combine flour, baking powder, soda, salt, coconut, oats, pecans, raisins, lemon rind, and orange rind in a medium mixing bowl; mix well. Add to creamed mixture; blend well. Drop dough by teaspoonfuls 2 inches apart onto ungreased cookie sheets. Bake at 375° for 10 to 12 minutes. Remove to wire racks to cool. Store in airtight containers. Yield: 4 dozen.

FROSTED APRICOT JEWELS

1¼ cups all-purpose flour
¼ cup sugar
1½ teaspoons baking powder
¼ teaspoon salt
½ cup butter or margarine,
    softened
1 (3-ounce) package cream cheese,
    softened
½ cup flaked coconut
½ cup apricot preserves
    Frosting (recipe follows)
    Pecan halves

Combine flour, sugar, baking powder, and salt in a medium mixing bowl; cut in butter and cream cheese with a pastry blender until mixture resembles coarse meal. Add coconut and preserves, mixing well.

Drop dough by heaping teaspoonfuls 2 inches apart onto ungreased cookie sheets. Bake at 350° for 15 to 18 minutes or until lightly browned. Cool completely on wire racks. Spread each cookie with frosting, and top with a pecan half. Yield: about 3 dozen.

Frosting:

1 cup sifted powdered sugar
1 tablespoon butter or margarine,
    softened
¼ cup apricot preserves

Combine all ingredients; beat until well blended. Yield: frosting for about 3 dozen cookies.

CHERRY DROP COOKIES

½ cup butter or margarine
1 (3-ounce) package cream cheese
1 cup sugar
2 eggs
1 teaspoon vanilla extract
1 teaspoon almond extract
2¼ cups all-purpose flour
2 teaspoons baking powder
1 teaspoon baking soda
½ teaspoon salt
1 (8½-ounce) can crushed
    pineapple, well drained
½ cup chopped maraschino
    cherries
1 cup chopped pecans (optional)

Cream butter and cream cheese; add sugar, beating until light and fluffy. Add eggs, one at a time, beating well after each addition. Stir in flavorings.

Combine flour, baking powder, soda, and salt in a medium mixing bowl. Gradually add to creamed mixture. Stir in pineapple, chopped cherries, and pecans, if desired. Drop dough by heaping tablespoonfuls 2 inches apart onto ungreased cookie sheets. Bake at 375° for 12 minutes. Remove to wire racks to cool. Yield: 2 dozen.

BANANA CAKE COOKIES

½ cup shortening
1 cup firmly packed brown sugar
2 eggs
1 cup mashed ripe banana
2 cups all-purpose flour
2 teaspoons baking powder
½ teaspoon baking soda
½ teaspoon salt
½ teaspoon ground cinnamon
½ teaspoon ground cloves
½ cup chopped pecans
    Powdered Sugar Icing

Cream shortening; add sugar, beating well. Add eggs and banana; beat well.

Sift together flour, baking powder, soda, salt, and spices. Add to creamed mixture; mix well. Stir in pecans.

Drop dough by tablespoonfuls 2 inches apart onto greased cookies sheets. Bake at 350° for 12 minutes. Remove to wire racks to cool. Spread tops of cooled cookies with Powdered Sugar Icing. Yield: about 3½ dozen.

Powdered Sugar Icing:

3 cups sifted powdered sugar
1 tablespoon butter or margarine,
    melted
¾ teaspoon vanilla extract
3 to 6 tablespoons milk

Combine first 3 ingredients in a medium mixing bowl; add milk to yield desired consistency, beating until smooth. Yield: icing for about 3½ dozen cookies.

COCONUT ISLAND COOKIES

3 (1-ounce) squares unsweetened
    chocolate
¼ cup strong coffee
½ cup shortening
1 cup firmly packed brown sugar
1 egg
2 cups all-purpose flour
½ teaspoon baking soda
½ teaspoon salt
⅔ cup commercial sour cream
1 cup flaked coconut, divided
    Chocolate Frosting

Heat chocolate and coffee in top of a double boiler over simmering water, stirring until chocolate melts. Set aside to cool.

Cream shortening in a large mixing bowl; gradually add sugar, beating well. Add egg and reserved chocolate mixture; beat well.

Combine flour, soda, and salt in a medium mixing bowl; add to creamed mixture alternately with sour cream, beginning and ending with flour mixture. Stir in ⅓ cup coconut.

Drop dough by heaping teaspoonfuls onto greased cookie sheets. Bake at 375° for 12 to 15 minutes. Spread chocolate frosting over tops of cookies while warm; sprinkle remaining coconut over frosting. Cool on cookie sheets until frosting sets. Store in airtight containers. Yield: about 6 dozen.

Chocolate Frosting:

1½ (1-ounce) squares unsweetened chocolate
¼ cup commercial sour cream
1 tablespoon butter or margarine
1 to 1½ cups sifted powdered sugar

Cook chocolate, sour cream, and butter in top of a double boiler over simmering water, stirring until chocolate and butter melt. Remove from heat, and stir in enough powdered sugar to yield desired spreading consistency. If necessary, reheat occasionally to maintain consistency. Yield: frosting for about 6 dozen cookies.

DATE-NUT COOKIES

1 cup chopped pecans or walnuts
1 cup chopped dates
1 cup chopped candied cherries
¼ cup all-purpose flour
¼ cup milk
1 teaspoon cider vinegar
½ cup butter, softened
1 cup firmly packed brown sugar
1 egg
1½ cups all-purpose flour
½ teaspoon baking soda
¼ teaspoon salt

Combine pecans, dates, cherries, and ¼ cup flour, tossing well. Combine milk and vinegar; let stand 10 minutes.

Cream butter; gradually add sugar, beating well. Add egg, beating well. Combine 1½ cups flour, soda, and salt in a small mixing bowl. Add to creamed mixture alternately with milk mixture, beginning and ending with flour mixture. Stir in fruit mixture.

Drop dough by heaping teaspoonfuls 2 inches apart onto ungreased cookie sheets. Bake at 375° for 10 minutes or until lightly browned. Remove from cookie sheets immediately, and cool on wire racks. Store in airtight containers. Yield: about 4 dozen.

SOUR CREAM DATE COOKIES

2 (8-ounce) packages pitted dates
2 cups pecan or walnut halves
¼ cup butter or margarine
¾ cup firmly packed brown sugar
1 egg
1¼ cups all-purpose flour
½ teaspoon baking powder
½ teaspoon baking soda
¼ teaspoon salt
½ cup commercial sour cream
Golden Frosting (optional)

Stuff each date with a pecan half.

Cream butter; gradually add sugar, beating well. Add egg; beat well.

Combine flour, baking powder, soda, and salt in a medium mixing bowl; add to creamed mixture alternately with sour cream, beginning and ending with flour mixture. Fold in prepared dates.

Drop dough by heaping teaspoonfuls 2 inches apart onto greased cookie sheets, allowing 1 date per cookie. Bake at 375° for 8 minutes or until lightly browned. Remove to wire racks to cool. Spread Golden Frosting over each cookie, if desired. Yield: 5½ dozen.

Golden Frosting:

½ cup butter
3 cups sifted powdered sugar
1 teaspoon vanilla extract
2 to 3 tablespoons water

Brown butter slightly in a medium skillet; remove from heat. Gradually add sugar and vanilla, beating well. Slowly add water, beating to yield desired spreading consistency. Yield: frosting for 5½ dozen cookies.

SPICY DATE COOKIES

⅔ cup shortening
1 cup sugar
2 eggs
1 teaspoon baking soda
¼ cup warm water
2 cups all-purpose flour
¼ teaspoon salt
¾ teaspoon ground
   cinnamon
¼ teaspoon ground cloves
2 (8-ounce) packages chopped
   dates
1 cup chopped pecans

Cream shortening in a large mixing bowl; gradually add sugar, beating until light and fluffy. Add eggs, one at a time, beating until well blended. Dissolve soda in warm water; stir into creamed mixture, blending well.

Sift together flour, salt, cinnamon, and cloves in a medium mixing bowl; add dates and pecans, stirring to coat well. Add to creamed mixture, stirring until thoroughly blended.

Drop dough by heaping teaspoonfuls 2 inches apart onto lightly greased cookie sheets. Bake at 350° for 12 to 14 minutes. Remove to wire racks to cool. Store in airtight containers. Yield: about 7½ dozen.

FIG DROP COOKIES

1 cup dried figs
½ cup shortening
¾ cup sugar
1 egg
½ cup molasses
¾ teaspoon vanilla extract
2 cups all-purpose flour
1 teaspoon baking soda
¼ teaspoon salt
½ teaspoon ground cinnamon
½ teaspoon ground ginger
½ cup chopped pecans

Combine figs and warm water to cover in a small mixing bowl; let stand 30 minutes. Drain and chop. Set aside.

Cream shortening in a large mixing bowl; gradually add sugar, beating until light and fluffy. Add egg, molasses, and vanilla; beat well.

Sift together flour, soda, salt, cinnamon, and ginger in a medium mixing bowl; add reserved figs and chopped pecans, stirring to coat well. Gradually stir flour mixture into creamed mixture; mix until well blended.

Drop dough by teaspoonfuls 2 inches apart onto greased cookie sheets. Bake at 350° for 10 minutes or until lightly browned. Cool slightly on cookie sheets; remove to wire racks to cool completely. Store in airtight containers. Yield: about 8 dozen.

EASY FRUITCAKE COOKIES

½ cup butter or margarine
1 cup firmly packed light brown
   sugar
4 eggs, beaten
3 cups all-purpose flour,
   divided
1 teaspoon baking soda
¾ teaspoon ground
   cardamom
2 cups chopped pecans
1 (8-ounce) package candied
   pineapple, chopped
¼ pound candied orange rind,
   chopped
¼ pound candied lemon rind,
   chopped

Cream butter in a large mixing bowl; gradually add sugar, beating well. Add eggs, one at a time, beating well after each addition. Add 2½ cups flour, mixing until well blended.

Combine ½ cup flour, soda, and cardamom in a large mixing bowl; add pecans and chopped candied fruit, tossing well to coat. Add to creamed mixture, and blend well.

Drop dough by teaspoonfuls 2 inches apart onto greased cookie sheets. Bake at 275° for 12 to 15 minutes. Remove to wire racks to cool. Store in airtight containers. Yield: 5 dozen.

FRUITCAKE COOKIES

1 cup shortening
2 cups firmly packed brown sugar
2 eggs
4 cups all-purpose flour
1 teaspoon baking soda
1 teaspoon salt
⅔ cup buttermilk
1 cup chopped pecans
1 cup candied cherries, cut into
    quarters
2 cups chopped dates
1 cup chopped candied fruit and
    peel
  Red or green cherry halves
  Pecan halves

Cream shortening; gradually add sugar, beating well. Add eggs; beat well.

Sift together flour, soda, and salt in a medium mixing bowl. Add to creamed mixture alternately with buttermilk, beginning and ending with flour mixture. Add pecans, quartered cherries, dates, and candied fruit and peel. Chill dough several hours or overnight.

Drop dough by teaspoonfuls 2 inches apart onto lightly greased cookie sheets. Top each cookie with a cherry or pecan half. Bake at 375° for 8 to 10 minutes. Remove to wire racks to cool. Yield: about 7 dozen.

CHRISTMAS FRUITCAKE COOKIES

1 cup butter, softened
1½ cups sugar
2 eggs
2½ cups all-purpose flour
1 teaspoon baking soda
½ teaspoon salt
1 teaspoon ground cinnamon
2 (8-ounce) packages chopped
    pitted dates
3 cups chopped pecans
1 (8-ounce) package candied yellow
    pineapple, chopped
1 (8-ounce) package candied red
    cherries, cut into quarters

Cream butter; gradually add sugar, beating until light and fluffy. Add eggs; beat well.

Combine flour, soda, salt, and cinnamon in a medium mixing bowl; gradually add to creamed mixture, beating well. Stir in the remaining ingredients.

Drop dough by heaping teaspoonfuls 2 inches apart onto lightly greased cookie sheets. Bake at 375° for 13 minutes or until lightly browned. Cool on cookie sheets 1 minute; remove to wire racks to cool completely. Yield: about 7 dozen.

LIZZIES

1 cup butter or margarine
1 cup firmly packed brown sugar
4 eggs
2½ cups all-purpose flour
1 teaspoon ground allspice
    (optional)
1 teaspoon ground cinnamon
    (optional)
1 teaspoon ground nutmeg
    (optional)
1 teaspoon baking soda
3 tablespoons milk
⅔ cup bourbon
1 pound chopped raisins or
    chopped dates
1 (8-ounce) package candied
    cherries, chopped
1 (8-ounce) package candied
    pineapple, chopped
2 cups chopped pecans

Cream butter in a large mixing bowl; gradually add sugar, beating until light and fluffy. Add eggs, one at a time, beating well after each addition.

Combine flour and spices, if desired; dissolve soda in milk. Add flour mixture to creamed mixture alternately with milk mixture and bourbon, beginning and ending with flour mixture. Add candied fruit and pecans, stirring well.

Drop dough by teaspoonfuls 2 inches apart onto greased cookie sheets. Bake at 250° for 15 to 20 minutes. Remove to wire racks to cool. Yield: about 6 dozen.

CARROT-ORANGE COOKIES

¾ cup shortening
¾ cup sugar
1 cup mashed, cooked
   carrots
1 egg
1 teaspoon vanilla extract
¾ teaspoon orange extract
2 cups all-purpose flour
2 teaspoons baking powder
¼ teaspoon salt
½ cup raisins
½ cup chopped pecans

Cream shortening in a large mixing bowl; gradually add sugar, beating until light and fluffy. Add carrots, egg, vanilla, and orange extract; beat well.

Combine flour, baking powder, and salt in a medium mixing bowl; add to creamed mixture, stirring well. Stir in raisins and pecans.

Drop dough by heaping teaspoonfuls 2 inches apart onto greased cookie sheets. Bake at 350° for 12 to 15 minutes. Remove to wire racks to cool. Yield: about 7 dozen.

FROSTED ORANGE COOKIES

1 cup shortening
2 cups sugar
2 eggs
4½ cups all-purpose flour
½ teaspoon baking powder
1 teaspoon baking soda
   Dash of salt
1 cup buttermilk
   Grated rind of 2 oranges,
    divided
⅔ cup orange juice, divided
1 (16-ounce) package powdered
   sugar, sifted

Cream shortening in a large mixing bowl; gradually add 2 cups sugar, beating well. Add eggs; beat well.

Sift together flour, baking powder, soda, and salt in a medium mixing bowl; add to creamed mixture alternately with buttermilk, beginning and ending with flour mixture. Beat well after each addition. Stir in half of grated rind and ⅓ cup orange juice, mixing well.

Drop dough by teaspoonfuls 2 inches apart onto greased cookie sheets. Bake at 375° for 10 minutes. Remove from cookie sheets, and cool completely on wire racks.

Combine remaining orange rind, juice, and powdered sugar in a medium mixing bowl, beating with a wire whisk until smooth; spread evenly over tops of cooled cookies. Yield: about 8½ dozen.

PUMPKIN SPICE COOKIES

½ cup shortening
1⅓ cups sugar
2 eggs
1 cup mashed, cooked
   pumpkin
1 teaspoon vanilla extract
½ teaspoon lemon extract
1 teaspoon grated lemon rind
2½ cups all-purpose flour
1 tablespoon baking powder
1 teaspoon salt
1 teaspoon ground cinnamon
1 teaspoon ground nutmeg
½ teaspoon ground allspice
¼ teaspoon ground ginger
1 cup raisins
½ cup chopped pecans
   Lemon Buttercream Frosting
   (optional)

Cream shortening in a large mixing bowl; gradually add sugar, beating well. Add eggs; beat until well blended. Stir in pumpkin, vanilla, lemon extract, and grated lemon rind.

Combine flour, baking powder, salt, and spices in a medium mixing bowl; stir well. Gradually add to creamed mixture, stirring well. Stir in raisins and pecans.

Drop dough by teaspoonfuls 2 inches apart onto greased cookie sheets. Bake at 375° for 12 minutes or until lightly browned. Remove to wire racks to cool. Frost with Lemon Buttercream Frosting, if desired. Yield: 7 dozen.

Lemon Buttercream Frosting:

¼ cup butter, softened
2¼ cups sifted powdered sugar,
    divided
3 tablespoons half-and-half
½ teaspoon grated lemon rind

Cream butter in medium mixing bowl; gradually add 1 cup powdered sugar, beating until well blended. Add remaining powdered sugar alternately with half-and-half, beating until smooth. Add lemon rind, and beat well. Yield: frosting for 7 dozen cookies.

GERMAN PECAN BRITTLES

1 cup shortening
1 cup sugar
1 cup firmly packed brown sugar
2 eggs
2 cups all-purpose flour
1 teaspoon baking powder
1 teaspoon baking soda
1 teaspoon salt
1 cup corn flakes cereal, crushed
1 cup chopped pecans
1 teaspoon vanilla extract

Cream shortening in a large mixing bowl; gradually add sugar, beating well. Add eggs; beat well.

Sift together flour, baking powder, soda, and salt in a medium mixing bowl; add crushed cereal and pecans, stirring to coat well. Add to creamed mixture, mixing until well blended. Stir in vanilla, blending well.

Drop dough by teaspoonfuls 2 inches apart onto greased and floured cookie sheets. Bake at 325° for 10 to 12 minutes. Remove to wire racks to cool. Yield: about 11 dozen.

PECAN CRISPIES

2 egg whites
1 cup firmly packed brown
    sugar
¼ cup all-purpose flour
2 cups pecan halves

Beat egg whites (at room temperature) in a medium mixing bowl until stiff peaks form. Gradually sprinkle sugar over beaten whites; continue to beat until well blended. Fold in flour and pecans.

Drop dough by teaspoonfuls 2 inches apart onto greased and floured cookie sheets. Bake at 300° for 20 to 25 minutes. Remove to wire racks to cool. Yield: about 4 dozen.

WALNUT WAFERS

2 eggs
1⅓ cups firmly packed brown
    sugar
¼ cup plus 1 tablespoon
    all-purpose flour
⅛ teaspoon baking powder
⅛ teaspoon salt
1 teaspoon vanilla extract
1 cup chopped walnuts

Beat eggs in a medium mixing bowl until thickened and tripled in volume; gradually add sugar, beating well. Add flour, baking powder, salt, and vanilla, mixing well. Stir in walnuts.

Drop dough by teaspoonfuls 2 inches apart onto parchment- or aluminum foil-lined cookie sheets. Bake at 375° for 6 minutes or until lightly browned. Cool completely on cookie sheets; store in airtight containers. Yield: about 5 dozen.

ROLLED AND SLICED COOKIES

BUTTER PECAN SHORTBREAD COOKIES

1 cup butter, softened
½ cup firmly packed brown sugar
2¼ cups all-purpose flour
½ cup finely chopped pecans

Cream butter; add sugar, beating until light and fluffy. Add flour, mixing well. Stir in pecans. Divide dough in half. Cover; chill 1 hour.

Roll one portion of dough to ¼-inch thickness between 2 sheets of waxed paper; keep remaining dough chilled until ready to use. Cut dough into desired shapes with 2-inch cutters; remove excess dough. Place a greased cookie sheet on top of cookies, greased side down. Invert cookie sheet, allowing cookies to transfer to sheet; remove waxed paper. Bake at 300° for 18 to 20 minutes or until lightly browned. Remove to wire racks to cool. Repeat rolling, cutting, and baking procedure with remaining dough. Yield: about 3 dozen.

VANILLA BEAN COOKIES

1 vanilla bean, finely diced
1 cup sifted powdered sugar
2 cups butter, softened
1 cup sugar
1 teaspoon vanilla extract
4 cups all-purpose flour
2¼ cups ground pecans (about ½ pound)

Combine diced vanilla bean and powdered sugar in an airtight container; let stand 3 days.

Cream butter in a large mixing bowl; gradually add 1 cup sugar, beating until light and fluffy. Stir in vanilla. Add flour and pecans, mixing well. Chill dough overnight.

Let dough stand until soft enough to roll. Roll to ⅛-inch thickness on a floured surface; cut into desired shapes. Place 2 inches apart on lightly greased cookie sheets. Bake at 350° for 12 minutes; remove to wire racks to cool. Sift vanilla-flavored powdered sugar evenly over cookies while warm. Yield: about 6 dozen.

SAND TARTS

1 cup butter or margarine
2 cups sugar
2 eggs
1 egg, separated
2 teaspoons vanilla extract
4 cups all-purpose flour
Cinnamon
Additional sugar

Cream butter in a large mixing bowl; gradually add 2 cups sugar, beating well. Add eggs and egg yolk; beat well. Stir in vanilla. Add flour; mix well.

Roll to ¼-inch thickness on a lightly floured surface. Cut with a 2½-inch round cutter. Beat egg white lightly; brush over cookies. Combine cinnamon and additional sugar; sprinkle over cookies. Place 2 inches apart on greased cookie sheets. Bake at 350° for 8 to 10 minutes. Remove to wire racks. Yield: about 6 dozen.

CARAMEL SAND TARTS

½ cup butter, softened
1 cup firmly packed brown sugar
1 egg
1 teaspoon vanilla extract
1½ cups all-purpose flour
2 teaspoons baking powder
¼ teaspoon salt
1 egg white
1 tablespoon sugar
¼ teaspoon ground cinnamon
  Pecan halves

Cream butter in a large mixing bowl; gradually add brown sugar, beating well. Add egg and vanilla; mix until well blended.

Combine flour, baking powder, and salt in a medium mixing bowl; add to creamed mixture, mixing well. Cover and chill 1 to 2 hours.

Roll dough to ⅛-inch thickness on a lightly floured surface; cut with a 2½-inch round cutter. Brush each cookie lightly with egg white. Combine sugar and cinnamon; sprinkle lightly over cookies. Place cookies 2 inches apart on lightly greased cookie sheets; gently press a pecan half in center of each. Bake at 350° for 8 to 10 minutes or until lightly browned. Remove to wire racks to cool. Store in airtight containers. Yield: 2½ dozen.

MORAVIAN TEA CAKES

½ cup butter, softened
1 cup sugar
3 eggs
1½ teaspoons vanilla extract
½ teaspoon lemon extract
3 cups all-purpose flour
2 teaspoons baking powder
½ teaspoon salt
¾ teaspoon ground nutmeg

Cream butter in a large mixing bowl; gradually add sugar, beating well. Add eggs, one at a time, beating well after each addition. Stir in vanilla and lemon extract.

Sift together flour, baking powder, salt, and nutmeg in a medium mixing bowl. Gradually add to creamed mixture, stirring well.

Roll dough to ⅛-inch thickness on a heavily floured surface; cut with assorted 2-inch cutters. Place 2 inches apart on lightly greased cookie sheets. Bake at 350° for 8 minutes or until lightly browned. Remove to wire racks to cool. Store in airtight containers. Yield: about 5½ dozen.

MOCHA JUMBLES

2 tablespoons shortening
½ cup sugar
1 egg
1 tablespoon cold water
1 (1-ounce) square unsweetened
  chocolate, melted
1½ cups all-purpose flour
2 teaspoons baking
  powder
1 tablespoon instant coffee
  granules
½ teaspoon ground cinnamon
  Additional sugar

Cream shortening in a large mixing bowl; gradually add ½ cup sugar, beating well. Add egg and water, beating until well blended. Stir in slightly cooled chocolate.

Combine flour, baking powder, coffee, and cinnamon in a small mixing bowl. Add to creamed mixture, stirring well. Wrap dough in waxed paper; refrigerate until firm.

Roll dough to ⅛-inch thickness on a lightly floured surface. Cut with a doughnut or round cutter. Sprinkle lightly with additional sugar. Place 2 inches apart on greased cookie sheets. Bake at 350° for 10 minutes. Remove to wire racks to cool. Store in airtight containers. Yield: 2½ dozen.

SWISS ALMOND CHRISTMAS WAFERS

1½ cups lightly toasted sliced
    almonds
½ cup sugar
2 teaspoons grated orange
    rind
½ cup butter or margarine,
    softened
1 egg
2 egg yolks
2 tablespoons amaretto
2¼ cups all-purpose
    flour
¼ teaspoon salt
1 egg yolk
1 tablespoon water
    Additional sugar
    Silver candy decorations or other
    decorator candies

Combine almonds, ½ cup sugar, and orange rind in container of a food processor or electric blender; process until almonds are finely ground.

Cream butter in a large mixing bowl, beating until well blended. Add almond mixture, beating well. Add egg, 2 egg yolks, and amaretto; beat until light and fluffy.

Combine flour and salt in a medium mixing bowl; add to creamed mixture, and mix until well blended. Shape dough into a ball; wrap in waxed paper, and chill until firm.

Roll dough to ¼-inch thickness between 2 sheets of waxed paper. (Turn dough over frequently to allow dough to spread.) Cut with a 2-inch round cutter, rerolling scraps of dough. Place ½-inch apart on greased and floured cookie sheets.

Combine 1 egg yolk and water in a small mixing bowl, blending well; brush mixture evenly over tops of cookies. Sprinkle additional sugar lightly over cookies, and decorate, as desired, with silver candy decorations. Bake at 350° for 15 to 18 minutes or until browned around edges. Remove to wire racks to cool; store in airtight containers. Yield: about 5½ dozen.

DECORATED SUGAR COOKIES

½ cup butter or margarine,
    softened
¾ cup sugar
1 egg
¾ teaspoon vanilla extract
2 cups all-purpose flour
½ teaspoon baking soda
½ teaspoon salt
    Royal Icing

Cream butter in a large mixing bowl; add sugar, beating until light and fluffy. Add egg and vanilla, mixing well.

Combine flour, soda, and salt; add to creamed mixture, blending well. (Dough will be very stiff.)

Divide dough into thirds; roll each portion to ⅛-inch thickness on lightly floured waxed paper. Cut with desired cutters, and place 2 inches apart on lightly greased cookie sheets. Bake at 375° for 8 to 10 minutes or until lightly browned. Remove to wire racks to cool.

Spoon red Royal Icing into a pastry bag fitted with a No. 3 round tip, and pipe outlines on cookies. Fill in between outlines by piping green connecting stars, using a No. 16 or No. 18 metal tip. Let icing dry. Yield: about 5 dozen.

Royal Icing:

3 egg whites
½ teaspoon cream of tartar
1 (16-ounce) package powdered
    sugar, sifted
    Red and green paste food
    coloring

Beat egg whites (at room temperature) and cream of tartar in a large mixing bowl at medium speed of an electric mixer until foamy; gradually add sugar, mixing well. Beat 5 to 7 minutes. Tint one-fourth of icing red; tint remaining icing green. Yield: icing for about 5 dozen cookies.

Note: Icing dries very quickly; keep covered at all times with plastic wrap. Food coloring may be substituted or omitted if icing is used for other cookie recipes.

OLD-FASHIONED CHRISTMAS COOKIES

1 cup butter or margarine, softened
2 cups sugar
¼ cup firmly packed brown sugar
2 eggs
¼ cup plus 2 tablespoons milk
2 teaspoons vanilla extract
4 cups all-purpose flour
2 teaspoons baking powder
½ teaspoon salt
Decorator candies
Royal Icing (page 40)

Cream butter. Add sugar and eggs, beating well. Stir in milk and vanilla.

Combine flour, baking powder, and salt in a large mixing bowl; add to creamed mixture, mixing well. Chill.

Roll dough to ⅛-inch thickness on a lightly floured surface; cut with assorted cutters. Place 2 inches apart on greased cookie sheets. Bake at 350° for 10 to 12 minutes. Remove to wire racks to cool.

Decorate, as desired, with candies and Royal Icing. Yield: about 5 dozen.

PAINTED CHRISTMAS COOKIES

½ cup butter or margarine, softened
½ cup shortening
1 cup sifted powdered sugar
1 egg
1 teaspoon vanilla extract
2½ cups all-purpose flour
1 teaspoon salt
Egg Yolk Paint

Cream butter and shortening; gradually add sugar, beating until light and fluffy. Add egg and vanilla; beat well.

Combine flour and salt; stir into creamed mixture. Divide dough in half; cover and chill at least 1 hour.

Roll one portion of dough to ⅛-inch thickness on a lightly floured cookie sheet. Cut with assorted cutters; remove excess dough. Paint assorted designs on cookies with Egg Yolk Paint, using a small paintbrush. Bake at 375° for 9 to 10 minutes. Remove to wire racks to cool. Repeat procedure with remaining dough. Yield: 2½ dozen.

Egg Yolk Paint:

1 egg yolk
¼ teaspoon water
Assorted colors of paste food coloring

Combine egg yolk and water; mix well. Divide mixture into several custard cups; tint as desired with paste food coloring. Cover until ready to use. If paint thickens, add a few drops of water and mix well. Yield: 1½ tablespoons.

LEMON ROLL-AND-CUT COOKIES

1 cup butter
1 cup sugar
2 egg yolks
1 teaspoon grated lemon rind
2 teaspoons fresh lemon juice
1 teaspoon vanilla extract
2 cups all-purpose flour
1 egg white
Ground almonds or pecans

Cream butter in large mixing bowl; gradually add sugar, beating until light and fluffy. Add egg yolks, lemon rind, juice, and vanilla, blending well. Add flour; beat well. Divide dough into fourths. Cover with waxed paper, and chill 2 hours or until firm.

Work with one portion of dough at a time, keeping remaining dough chilled until ready to use. Roll to ¼-inch thickness on a lightly floured surface. Cut into desired shapes with 2-inch cutters. Place 1 inch apart on ungreased cookie sheets; brush with egg white, and sprinkle with ground almonds or pecans. Bake at 325° for 15 to 20 minutes or until edges are lightly browned. Remove to wire racks to cool. Repeat procedure with remaining dough. Yield: about 5 dozen.

LEMON GINGER COOKIES

¾ cup butter or margarine
½ cup sugar
1 egg, beaten
2 teaspoons grated lemon
    rind
1 tablespoon fresh lemon
    juice
⅓ cup finely chopped candied
    ginger
3 cups all-purpose flour
1 teaspoon baking powder
¼ teaspoon salt

Cream butter; gradually add sugar, beating until light and fluffy. Stir in egg, lemon rind, juice, and ginger.

Combine flour, baking powder, and salt in a medium mixing bowl; add to creamed mixure, mixing well. Divide dough in half; cover and chill slightly.

Roll one portion of dough to ⅛-inch thickness on a lightly floured surface; keep remaining dough chilled until ready to use. Cut with floured cutters into desired shapes. Place 2 inches apart on greased cookie sheets. Bake at 425° for 6 to 8 minutes or until lightly browned. Remove to wire racks to cool. Repeat procedure with remaining dough. Yield: 5 dozen.

EARLY AMERICAN GINGER CUTOUTS

½ cup butter or margarine
½ cup firmly packed dark
    brown sugar
¾ cup dark molasses
1 egg, beaten
2¾ cups all-purpose flour
½ teaspoon baking soda
½ teaspoon salt
1 teaspoon ground ginger
½ teaspoon ground
    cinnamon
½ teaspoon ground cloves
1 teaspoon hot water
1 teaspoon vinegar

Cream butter in a large mixing bowl; gradually add sugar, beating until light and fluffy. Add molasses and egg; beat until smooth.

Sift together flour, soda, salt, and spices; add to creamed mixture, stirring well. Add water and vinegar, blending well. Chill 2 hours or overnight.

Roll dough to ¼-inch thickness on a lightly floured surface; cut with assorted cutters. Place 2 inches apart on greased cookie sheets. Bake at 350° for 15 minutes. Remove to wire racks to cool; decorate as desired. Yield: about 2½ dozen.

GINGERBREAD COOKIES

½ cup butter or margarine,
    softened
½ cup firmly packed brown sugar
½ cup molasses
1 egg
3½ cups all-purpose flour
1 teaspoon baking powder
½ teaspoon baking soda
½ teaspoon salt
1 teaspoon ground cinnamon
½ teaspoon ground ginger
¼ teaspoon ground nutmeg
¼ teaspoon ground cloves
½ cup buttermilk
    Royal Icing (page 40)
    Currants

Cream butter; gradually add sugar, beating until light and fluffy. Add molasses and egg, mixing well.

Combine flour, baking powder, soda, salt, and spices, mixing well. Add to creamed mixture alternately with buttermilk, beginning and ending with flour mixture. Shape into a ball; cover and chill 2 hours.

Roll dough to ¼-inch thickness on a lightly floured surface; cut into desired shapes. Place 2 inches apart on lightly greased cookie sheets. Bake at 375° for 10 minutes. Remove to wire racks to cool. Decorate, as desired, with Royal Icing and currants, using icing to attach currants. Store in airtight containers. Yield: about 3 dozen.

GINGERBREAD MEN

½ cup butter or margarine, softened
¾ cup sugar
1 egg
¼ cup molasses
Juice of ½ orange
3½ to 4 cups all-purpose flour
1 teaspoon baking soda
½ teaspoon salt
1 teaspoon ground cinnamon
1 teaspoon ground ginger
Raisins
Royal Icing (page 40)

Cream butter; gradually add sugar, beating until light and fluffy. Add egg, molasses, and orange juice; beat well.

Combine flour, soda, salt, and spices; add to creamed mixture, blending well. Divide dough in half; chill 1 hour or until stiff enough to handle.

Roll one portion of dough to ⅛-inch thickness on a greased cookie sheet; keep remaining half chilled until ready to use. Cut with a 2- or 5-inch gingerbread man cutter, and remove excess dough. Press several raisins into each cookie to make eyes, nose, and buttons. Bake at 350° for 10 minutes. Cool 1 minute on cookie sheets; remove to wire racks to cool completely. Repeat procedure with remaining dough. Decorate, as desired, with Royal Icing. Yield: about 3 dozen.

FRUIT AND NUT SPICE COOKIES

½ cup butter or margarine
½ cup sugar
½ cup molasses
2 tablespoons rum
2 tablespoons water
2½ cups all-purpose flour
½ teaspoon baking soda
½ teaspoon salt
½ teaspoon ground cinnamon
¼ teaspoon ground nutmeg
¼ teaspoon ground ginger
½ cup finely chopped pecans
½ cup candied fruit, finely chopped

Cream butter; add sugar, beating until light and fluffy. Stir in molasses, rum, water, flour, soda, salt, and spices. Add pecans and candied fruit; mix well. Cover and chill 2 to 3 hours.

Roll dough to ¼-inch thickness on a lightly floured surface. Cut with a 2½-inch round cutter; place 2 inches apart on ungreased cookie sheets. Bake at 350° for 10 minutes; remove to wire racks to cool. Yield: 3 dozen.

HALF-MOONS

1 cup lard
1 cup sugar
2 cups molasses
1 (8-ounce) carton commercial sour cream
1½ teaspoons baking soda
Dash of salt
1½ teaspoons ground cinnamon
1½ teaspoons ground allspice
1½ teaspoons ground cloves
1 cup chopped pecans
7 cups all-purpose flour

Cream lard in a large mixing bowl; gradually add sugar, beating until light and fluffy. Add molasses, sour cream, soda, salt, and spices; beat well. Stir in pecans. Add flour to form a stiff dough. Divide dough into fourths; cover and chill overnight.

Roll one portion of dough to ¼-inch thickness on a lightly floured surface; keep remaining dough chilled until ready to use. Cut with a half-moon cutter. Place 2 inches apart on lightly greased cookie sheets. Bake at 350° for 10 to 12 minutes. Remove to wire racks to cool. Repeat procedure with remaining dough. Store in airtight containers. Yield: about 15 dozen.

SWEDISH COOKIES

1 cup butter or margarine,
   softened
1 cup sugar
½ teaspoon vanilla extract
½ cup plus 2 tablespoons
   commercial sour cream
2½ cups all-purpose flour
¼ teaspoon salt
1 cup sifted powdered sugar
   Water
   Green and red food coloring

Cream butter in a large mixing bowl; gradually add 1 cup sugar, beating until light and fluffy. Add vanilla and sour cream, mixing well.

Combine flour and salt; fold into creamed mixture. Cover dough, and chill several hours or overnight.

Working with small portions of dough at a time, roll to ¼-inch thickness on a lightly floured surface. Cut with star- or tree-shaped cookie cutters. Place 1 inch apart on lightly greased cookie sheets. Bake at 350° for 8 to 10 minutes. Remove to wire racks to cool.

Combine powdered sugar and enough water to yield a thin spreading consistency. Tint two-thirds of mixture green and one-third red. Spread green mixture evenly over cookies; outline edges with red mixture.

SOUR CREAM COOKIES

1 cup shortening
1 cup sugar
1 egg
1 (8-ounce) carton commercial
   sour cream
1 teaspoon vanilla
   extract
4¾ cups all-purpose flour
1 teaspoon baking powder
1 teaspoon baking
   soda
¼ teaspoon salt
   Red and green decorator sugar
   crystals

Cream shortening; gradually add sugar, beating until light and fluffy. Add egg; beat until well blended. Stir in sour cream and vanilla, mixing well.

Combine flour, baking powder, soda, and salt; add to creamed mixture, beating well. Divide dough into thirds; cover and chill at least 1 hour.

Roll one portion of dough to ⅛-inch thickness on a lightly floured surface; keep remaining dough chilled until ready to use. Cut into desired shapes. Place 2 inches apart on ungreased cookie sheets; sprinkle with sugar crystals. Bake at 350° for 10 to 12 minutes or until lightly browned. Remove to wire racks to cool. Repeat procedure with remaining dough. Yield: about 8 dozen.

Note: Cookies may be decorated with Royal Icing (page 40) and assorted candies and sprinkles after baking and cooling. (Omit sugar crystals.)

CREAM CHEESE CRESCENTS

1 cup butter or margarine,
   softened
1 (8-ounce) package cream cheese,
   softened
2 cups all-purpose flour
¼ teaspoon salt
¾ cup finely chopped walnuts
⅓ cup sugar
1½ teaspoons ground cinnamon
   Sifted powdered sugar

Cream butter and cream cheese. Combine flour and salt; add to creamed mixture, mixing well. Shape dough into 8 balls; wrap each in plastic wrap, and chill at least 2 hours.

Roll each ball into an 8-inch circle on a lightly floured surface; cut each into 8 wedges. Combine walnuts, ⅓ cup sugar, and cinnamon; sprinkle ¼ teaspoon mixture over each wedge. Starting at wide edge of dough, roll up each wedge; shape into a crescent. Place point side down on ungreased cookie sheets. Bake at 350° for 12 minutes or until lightly browned; cool and dust with powdered sugar. Yield: about 5 dozen.

CREAM CHEESE HORNS

½ cup butter, softened
1 (3-ounce) package cream cheese,
   softened
1½ cups sifted cake flour
2 tablespoons sugar
½ teaspoon salt
1 tablespoon whipping cream
½ teaspoon vanilla extract
   Pineapple or raspberry jelly
½ cup finely chopped pecans
2 egg whites, lightly beaten
   Finely chopped pistachio nuts

Cream butter and cream cheese in a large mixing bowl, beating well.

Combine flour, sugar, and salt in a small mixing bowl. Add to creamed mixture, stirring well. Stir in whipping cream and vanilla; mix well. Cover and refrigerate overnight.

Roll dough to ⅛-inch thickness on a lightly floured surface; cut with a 2-inch round cutter. Place ¼ teaspoon jelly in center of each cookie; sprinkle with pecans. Fold opposite edges over filling and pinch together, forming a cornucopia. Brush open end of cornucopia with egg whites; sprinkle with pistachio nuts. Repeat procedure with remaining cookies, egg whites, and nuts. Place 2 inches apart on lightly greased cookies sheets. Bake at 325° for 15 minutes. Remove to wire racks to cool. Yield: about 4 dozen.

CHERRY DELECTABLES

1 cup butter, softened
1 (8-ounce) package cream cheese
2 cups all-purpose flour
2 (16-ounce) jars plus 1 (8-ounce)
   jar maraschino cherries,
   undrained
¼ cup brandy
   Sifted powdered sugar

Cream butter and cream cheese in a large mixing bowl; gradually add flour, blending until a stiff dough is formed. Chill 8 hours or overnight.

Drain cherries, reserving ¼ cup liquid. Combine cherries, reserved liquid, and brandy. Chill 8 hours or overnight.

Drain cherries well, discarding liquid. Divide dough in half, keeping one portion chilled until ready to use. Roll dough to ⅛-inch thickness on a surface sprinkled with powdered sugar. Cut into 3- x 1-inch strips. Place a cherry on each strip, and roll up, pinching end of strip to seal. (Cherry will be exposed on both sides of the pastry strip.) Place seam-side down on lightly greased cookie sheets. Bake at 350° for 15 minutes or until lightly browned. Remove from oven, and sprinkle with powdered sugar while warm. Remove to wire racks to cool. Yield: 10 dozen.

Note: Pecan halves may be substituted for cherries. (Omit soaking in brandy.)

BITTER CHOCOLATE COOKIES

¾ cup butter, softened
1 cup sugar
⅛ teaspoon salt
1 egg
4 (1-ounce) squares unsweetened
   chocolate, melted
1 teaspoon vanilla extract
1¾ cups all-purpose flour

Cream butter in a medium mixing bowl; gradually add sugar and salt, beating until light and fluffy. Add egg, beating well.

Stir melted chocolate and vanilla into creamed mixture. Add flour, stirring well; chill 1 hour.

Roll dough to ¼-inch thickness on a lightly floured surface. Cut with a 2-inch round cutter. Place 2 inches apart on lightly greased cookie sheets. Bake at 425° for 6 to 8 minutes. Cool slightly on cookie sheets; remove to wire racks to cool completely. Yield: about 4 dozen.

CHOCOLATE SANDWICH COOKIES

½ cup butter or margarine, softened
1¼ cups sugar
3 (1-ounce) squares unsweetened chocolate, melted
1 teaspoon vanilla extract
2 eggs
2½ cups all-purpose flour
1½ teaspoons baking powder
½ teaspoon baking soda
½ teaspoon salt
Filling (recipe follows)

Cream butter in a large mixing bowl; gradually add sugar, beating well. Add melted chocolate and vanilla; beat well. Add eggs, one at a time, beating well after each addition.

Combine flour, baking powder, soda, and salt in a medium mixing bowl. Add to creamed mixture, stirring well. Divide dough in half; wrap in waxed paper, and chill 1 hour.

Roll one portion of dough to ⅛-inch thickness on a lightly floured surface; keep remaining dough chilled until ready to use. Cut with a 2½-inch fluted or round cutter. Place 2 inches apart on ungreased cookie sheets. Bake at 350° for 8 to 10 minutes. Remove from cookie sheets; cool on wire racks. Repeat procedure with remaining dough, and cut out center of each cookie with a ½-inch round cutter before baking. Spread filling evenly over bottom of each solid cookie. Top with remaining cookies, bottom sides down, to make sandwiches; press down slightly to fill cut-outs. Yield: 1½ dozen.

Filling:

⅔ cup shortening
¼ teaspoon salt
½ teaspoon vanilla extract
⅓ cup water
1 (16-ounce) package powdered sugar, sifted

Combine shortening, salt, and vanilla in a medium mixing bowl; beat at medium speed of an electric mixer until well blended. Add small amounts of water alternately with sugar, beating at low speed until mixture is blended. Beat an additional 8 minutes at medium speed until smooth. Yield: filling for 1½ dozen cookies.

Note: Filling may be stored in a covered container at room temperature or in refrigerator several days.

DAISY DATE COOKIES

1 cup butter or margarine
1¼ cups sugar
1 egg
1 teaspoon vanilla extract
2½ cups all-purpose flour
1 cup regular or quick-cooking oats, uncooked
Date Filling

Cream butter in a large mixing bowl; gradually add sugar, beating until light and fluffy. Add egg and vanilla, beating until well blended.

Combine flour and oats in a medium mixing bowl; add to creamed mixture, stirring well. (Dough may be chilled for easy handling.)

Roll dough to ⅛-inch thickness on a lightly floured surface. Cut with a 2-inch fluted cutter. Cut out centers of half of cookies with a ¾-inch round cutter. Place cookies 2 inches apart on greased cookie sheets. Bake at 375° for 7 to 9 minutes. Remove to wire racks to cool.

Spread Date Filling evenly over bottom of each solid cookie. Top with remaining cookies, bottom sides down, to make sandwiches. Press lightly to fill cut-outs. Yield: about 3 dozen.

Date Filling:

  1 (8-ounce) package chopped
      dates
  ¾ cup water
  ¼ cup sugar
  2 tablespoons lemon
      juice

Combine all ingredients in a medium saucepan. Cook over low heat, stirring constantly, 10 minutes or until mixture thickens. Cool completely before spreading on cookies. Yield: filling for about 3 dozen cookies.

ITALIAN PILLOWS

  1 cup shortening
  1 cup sugar
  2 teaspoons vanilla extract
  ¼ teaspoon salt
  4 eggs
  4 hard-cooked egg yolks
  3¾ cups all-purpose flour
  ½ cup whipping
      cream
  1 (10-ounce) jar orange marmalade,
      divided
  1 egg white

Cream shortening in a large mixing bowl; gradually add sugar, beating until light and fluffy. Add vanilla and salt, beating well. Add 4 eggs, one at a time, beating well after each addition. Press hard-cooked egg yolks through a sieve onto creamed mixture; stir until well blended.

Add flour to creamed mixture alternately with whipping cream, beginning and ending with flour. Stir well after each addition. Cover and chill dough overnight.

Work with one-fourth of dough at a time, keeping remaining dough chilled until ready to use. Roll to ¼-inch thickness on a well-floured surface, and cut into 2-inch squares. Place ¼ teaspoon orange marmalade in center of each square. Fold dough into a triangle, and gently press edges together with tines of a fork. Brush tops of cookies with egg white. Place 2 inches apart on lightly greased cookie sheets. Bake at 350° for 15 minutes or until lightly browned. Remove to wire racks to cool completely. Repeat procedure with remaining dough, orange marmalade, and egg white. Store in airtight containers. Yield: about 8 dozen.

LINZER COOKIES

  1½ cups butter, softened
  1 cup sugar
  2 eggs
  1 teaspoon vanilla extract
  1 (14-ounce) package blanched
      whole almonds, finely ground
  3⅓ cups sifted cake flour
  1 teaspoon baking powder
  1 teaspoon ground cinnamon
      Raspberry jam
      Powdered sugar

Cream butter; gradually add 1 cup sugar, beating until light and fluffy. Add eggs and vanilla, beating well; stir in ground almonds, mixing well.

Sift together flour, baking powder, and cinnamon in a medium mixing bowl; gradually add to creamed mixture, stirring well. Divide dough into fourths; cover and refrigerate overnight.

Roll one portion of dough to ¼-inch thickness between 2 pieces of waxed paper; keep remaining dough chilled until ready to use. Cut with a 2-inch heart-shaped cutter; place half of cookies on lightly greased cookie sheets. Cut out centers of remaining cookies, using a ¾-inch round cutter; place on lightly greased cookie sheets. Bake at 350° for 10 to 12 minutes. Remove to wire racks to cool. Repeat procedure with remaining dough.

Spread a small amount of jam on bottom of each solid cookie. Top with remaining cookies, bottom sides down, to make sandwiches. Sift powdered sugar over tops of cookies. Fill cut-outs with jam. Store in airtight containers. Yield: about 2½ dozen.

CHRISTMAS FORTUNE COOKIES

2 cups butter, softened
1 cup sugar
6 cups all-purpose flour
    Royal Icing

Prepare 4½ dozen fortunes on 4- x 1-inch strips of paper; fold paper strips in half lengthwise, and set aside.

Cream butter in a large mixing bowl; gradually add sugar, beating until light and fluffy. Add flour to creamed mixture, mixing until well blended. (Dough will be dry.)

Working with a small amount of dough at a time, roll to ⅛-inch thickness on an unfloured surface, using a floured rolling pin. Cut with a 2½-inch doughnut cutter. Place 2 inches apart on ungreased cookie sheets. Bake at 400° for 5 to 7 minutes or until lightly browned. Remove to wire racks to cool.

Spoon green Royal Icing into a pastry bag fitted with a No. 75 tip. Pipe green leaves on top of half the cookies. Spoon red Royal Icing into a pastry bag fitted with a No. 3 tip. Pipe small red holly berries around leaves. Pipe red bows on cookies, using a No. 3 or No. 44 tip. Set cookies aside to dry.

Pipe a small strip of red icing at top and bottom of back side of remaining cookies. Lay a fortune across center of cookies. (Do not touch icing.) Top with decorated cookies, bottom sides down. Set cookies aside to dry. Yield: 4½ dozen.

Royal Icing:

3 egg whites
½ teaspoon cream of tartar
1 (16-ounce) package powdered sugar, sifted
    Red and green paste food coloring

Beat egg whites (at room temperature) and cream of tartar in a large mixing bowl at medium speed of an electric mixer until foamy; gradually add sugar, mixing well. Beat 5 to 7 minutes. Tint one-fourth of icing red; tint remaining icing green. Yield: icing for 4½ dozen cookies.

Note: Icing dries very quickly; keep covered at all times with plastic wrap. Food coloring may be substituted or omitted if icing is used for other recipes.

ALMOND ICEBOX COOKIES

2 cups butter or margarine, softened
2 cups sugar
4 cups all-purpose flour
2 teaspoons baking powder
1 teaspoon vanilla extract
1 egg white, lightly beaten
    Finely chopped almonds

Cream butter in a large mixing bowl; gradually add sugar, beating until light and fluffy.

Combine flour and baking powder in a medium mixing bowl; mix well. Add flour mixture and vanilla to creamed mixture, stirring well.

Shape dough into 2 rolls, 1½ inches in diameter. Wrap each roll in waxed paper, and refrigerate 2 hours. Remove waxed paper; cut rolls into ¼-inch slices. Place 2 inches apart on lightly greased cookie sheets. Brush lightly with egg white; sprinkle with almonds. Bake at 425° for 10 minutes or until lightly browned. Remove to wire racks to cool. Store in airtight containers. Yield: about 7½ dozen.

BUTTERSCOTCH COOKIES

1½ cups butter, softened
2 cups firmly packed brown sugar
2 eggs
3 cups all-purpose flour
2 teaspoons baking powder

Cream butter in a large mixing bowl; gradually add sugar, beating until light and fluffy. Add eggs; beat well. Stir in flour and baking powder, mixing well.

Shape dough into 2 rolls, 2 inches in

diameter. Wrap in waxed paper, and chill overnight or until firm. Remove waxed paper, and cut into ¼-inch slices. Place 2 inches apart on ungreased cookie sheets. Bake at 375° for 8 minutes or until lightly browned. Remove to wire racks to cool. Yield: about 7 dozen.

BUTTER CRISPS

 1 cup butter or margarine
1½ cups sifted powdered
      sugar
 3 cups all-purpose flour
 ¼ teaspoon salt
 1 egg, lightly beaten
 1 teaspoon vanilla extract
 1 cup chopped pecans

Cream butter; gradually add sugar, beating until light and fluffy.

Sift together flour and salt; add 1 cup flour mixture to creamed mixture, beating well. Add egg and vanilla, blending well. (Scrape bottom and sides of bowl often.) Add remaining flour mixture, beating well. Stir in pecans.

Shape dough into 2 rolls, 2 inches in diameter; wrap in waxed paper. Chill thoroughly. Remove waxed paper, and cut into ⅛-inch slices. Place 1 inch apart on lightly greased cookie sheets. Bake at 350° for 10 minutes or until edges are browned. Remove to wire racks to cool. Yield: about 9½ dozen.

COFFEE CRISPS

 ⅓ cup shortening
 ⅓ cup butter
 ⅓ cup sugar
 ½ cup firmly packed brown sugar
 1 egg
 1 teaspoon rum extract
 2 cups all-purpose flour
 ½ teaspoon baking powder
 ⅛ teaspoon baking soda
 ½ teaspoon salt
 2 tablespoons instant coffee
      granules
    Pecan halves

Cream shortening and butter in a large mixing bowl; gradually add sugar, beating until light and fluffy. Add egg; beat until well blended. Stir in rum extract, blending well.

Combine flour, baking powder, soda, salt, and coffee in a medium mixing bowl, stirring well. Add to creamed mixture; mix well.

Shape dough into 2 rolls, 2 inches in diameter; wrap in waxed paper, and chill 8 hours or overnight. Remove waxed paper, and cut into ⅛-inch slices. Place 1 inch apart on ungreased cookie sheets. Gently press a pecan half in center of each cookie. Bake at 400° for 8 to 10 minutes. Remove to wire racks to cool. Store in airtight containers. Yield: 6 dozen.

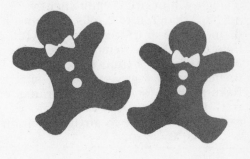

DUTCH CHEESE WAFERS

 ½ cup butter, softened
 1 (3-ounce) package cream cheese,
      softened
 ½ cup sugar
 1 cup all-purpose flour
 ½ cup finely chopped dried apricots
      or peaches

Cream butter and cream cheese in a medium mixing bowl; gradually add sugar, beating until light and fluffy. Stir in flour and apricots; mix well.

Shape dough into a roll, 1-inch in diameter. Wrap in waxed paper, and chill 3 hours or until firm. Remove waxed paper, and cut into ¼-inch slices. Place 1 inch apart on ungreased cookie sheets. Bake at 350° for 8 to 10 minutes. Remove to wire racks to cool. Yield: about 7 dozen.

NUTMEG REFRIGERATOR COOKIES

1 cup butter or margarine
⅔ cup sugar
⅔ cup firmly packed brown sugar
1 egg
1 teaspoon vanilla extract
3 cups all-purpose flour
1 tablespoon baking powder
¾ teaspoon salt
¼ teaspoon ground nutmeg

Cream butter; gradually add sugar, beating until light and fluffy. Add egg; beat well. Stir in vanilla.

Sift together flour, baking powder, salt, and nutmeg in a medium mixing bowl. Add to creamed mixture; mix well. (Dough will be stiff.) Chill slightly.

Shape dough into 2 rolls, 2 inches in diameter. Wrap in waxed paper; chill 1 hour or until firm. Remove waxed paper, and cut into ⅛-inch slices. Place 2 inches apart on greased cookie sheets. Bake at 400° for 10 to 12 minutes or until lightly browned. Remove to wire racks to cool. Store in airtight containers. Yield: 6 dozen.

SHAKER VANILLA COOKIES

½ cup butter or margarine, softened
¾ cup sugar
1 egg
1¼ teaspoons vanilla extract
1½ cups all-purpose flour
1 teaspoon baking powder
¼ teaspoon salt

Cream butter in a large mixing bowl; gradually add sugar, beating until light and fluffy. Add egg and vanilla, beating until well blended.

Sift together flour, baking powder, and salt in a medium mixing bowl; add to creamed mixture, mixing well.

Shape dough into a roll, 1½ inches in diameter; wrap in waxed paper, and chill 2 hours. Remove waxed paper, and cut into ¼-inch slices. Place 2 inches apart on lightly greased cookie sheets. Bake at 400° for 8 minutes. Remove to wire racks to cool. Yield: about 3 dozen.

VANILLA-NUT ICEBOX COOKIES

1 cup shortening
1 cup sugar
¼ cup firmly packed brown sugar
1 egg, beaten
2 teaspoons vanilla extract
1 cup chopped pecans
2 cups all-purpose flour
1½ teaspoons baking powder
¼ teaspoon salt

Cream shortening in a large mixing bowl; gradually add sugar, beating until light and fluffy. Add egg and vanilla; beat well. Stir in pecans.

Combine flour, baking powder, and salt in a medium mixing bowl; gradually add to creamed mixture, stirring well.

Shape dough into 2 rolls, 2 inches in diameter. Wrap each in waxed paper; chill until firm. Remove waxed paper, and cut into ¼-inch slices. Place 1 inch apart on ungreased cookie sheets. Bake at 425° for 5 minutes. Remove to wire racks to cool. Yield: about 5 dozen.

CHOCOLATE THINS

1 cup butter or margarine, softened
¾ cup light corn syrup
½ cup sugar
3 cups all-purpose flour
¾ cup cocoa
½ teaspoon baking powder
¼ teaspoon salt
1 cup chopped pecans

Cream butter in a large mixing bowl; gradually add syrup and sugar, beating until smooth.

Combine remaining ingredients in a medium mixing bowl, stirring well. Gradually add to creamed mixture, and mix well.

Shape dough into 2 rolls, 2 inches in diameter; wrap in waxed paper, and chill. Remove waxed paper, and cut into 1/8-inch slices. Place 1 inch apart on ungreased cookie sheets. Bake at 400° for 5 minutes. Remove to wire racks to cool. Yield: about 10 dozen.

CHOCOLATE SPIDERWEB SNAPS

4 (1-ounce) squares unsweetened
    chocolate
1 1/4 cups shortening
2 cups sugar
2 eggs
1/3 cup light corn syrup
2 tablespoons plus 1 1/2 teaspoons
    water
1 teaspoon vanilla extract
4 cups all-purpose flour
2 teaspoons baking soda
1/2 teaspoon salt
    Frosting (recipe follows)
1/2 cup semisweet chocolate morsels

Melt unsweetened chocolate in top of a double boiler over simmering water. Remove from heat.

Cream shortening in a large mixing bowl; gradually add sugar, beating until light and fluffy. Add melted chocolate, eggs, syrup, water, and vanilla; mix well.

Combine flour, soda, and salt; add to creamed mixture, blending well.

Shape dough into 2 rolls, 2 1/2 inches in diameter. Wrap in waxed paper, and chill 8 hours or overnight. Remove waxed paper, and cut into 1/4-inch slices. Place 1 inch apart on ungreased cookie sheets. Bake at 350° for 10 to 12 minutes. Cool on cookie sheets 5 minutes. Remove to wire racks to cool completely.

Spread frosting evenly over cookies to within 1/8-inch of edge; let stand until frosting sets.

Melt chocolate in top of a double boiler over simmering water; let stand just until cool, but not set. Spoon into a pastry bag fitted with a No. 2 round tip. Pipe chocolate in parallel lines, 1/4-inch apart, across tops of cookies. Pull the point of a wooden pick diagonally across lines. Let stand at room temperature until chocolate sets. Yield: 5 dozen.

Frosting:

6 cups sifted powdered sugar
1/4 cup plus 2 tablespoons warm
    water
    Paste food coloring

Combine sugar and enough water to yield desired spreading consistency, mixing well. Color, as desired, with a small amount of paste food coloring. Yield: frosting for 5 dozen cookies.

CHOCOLATE REFRIGERATOR COOKIES

1/3 cup butter or margarine
1/2 cup sugar
1/2 cup firmly packed brown sugar
1 egg
1 teaspoon vanilla extract
1 tablespoon milk
2 (1-ounce) squares chocolate,
    melted
2 cups all-purpose flour
1 teaspoon baking powder
1/4 teaspoon salt
1/2 cup chopped pecans

Cream butter in a large mixing bowl; gradually add sugar, beating well. Add egg; beat well. Stir in vanilla, milk, and melted chocolate; beat well.

Sift together flour, baking powder, and salt in a medium mixing bowl; stir in pecans. Add to creamed mixture, mixing well.

Shape dough into rolls, 1 1/2 inches in diameter. Wrap in waxed paper, and chill thoroughly. Remove waxed paper, and cut into 1/8-inch slices. Place 1 inch apart on ungreased cookie sheets. Bake at 425° for 5 to 7 minutes. Remove to wire racks to cool. Yield: 5 dozen.

Note: These cookies may be frozen before or after baking.

CHOCOLATE-WALNUT REFRIGERATOR COOKIES

1¼ cups butter or margarine, softened
1 cup sugar
2 eggs
4 (1-ounce) squares unsweetened chocolate, melted
1 teaspoon vanilla extract
3½ cups all-purpose flour
1 tablespoon baking powder
½ teaspoon salt
2 cups chopped walnuts

Cream butter; gradually add sugar, beating until light and fluffy. Add eggs; beat well. Add melted chocolate and vanilla, beating until well blended.

Combine flour, baking powder, and salt; add to creamed mixture, stirring well. Stir in walnuts.

Shape dough into 2 rolls, 2 inches in diameter. Cover and chill overnight. Cut into ⅛-inch slices. Place 2 inches apart on ungreased cookie sheets. Bake at 350° for 8 to 10 minutes. Remove to wire racks. Yield: about 13 dozen.

CHERRY REFRIGERATOR COOKIES

¾ cup butter or margarine
½ cup sugar
½ cup firmly packed brown sugar
2 eggs
2¾ cups all-purpose flour
1 teaspoon baking powder
¼ teaspoon baking soda
¼ teaspoon salt
½ teaspoon ground cinnamon
1 cup chopped candied cherries
1 cup chopped pecans

Cream butter in a large mixing bowl; gradually add sugar, beating until light and fluffy. Add eggs, and beat well.

Combine flour, baking powder, soda, salt, and cinnamon in a medium mixing bowl. Add to creamed mixture, stirring well. Stir in cherries and pecans.

Shape dough into 2 rolls, 1½ inches in diameter; wrap in waxed paper, and chill several hours or overnight. Remove waxed paper, and cut into ¼-inch slices. Place 1 inch apart on greased cookie sheets. Bake at 375° for 8 to 10 minutes or until lightly browned. Remove to wire racks to cool. Yield: 8 dozen.

COCONUT ICEBOX COOKIES

3 eggs, lightly beaten
1 cup sugar
½ cup firmly packed brown sugar
1½ cups shortening, melted
4 cups grated coconut
5½ cups sifted cake flour
1 tablespoon baking powder
¼ teaspoon salt

Combine eggs, sugar, melted shortening, and coconut in a large mixing bowl, and mix well.

Sift together flour, baking powder, and salt in a large mixing bowl. Add to egg mixture, stirring well.

Press dough into a waxed paper-lined 8-inch square baking pan; cover and refrigerate overnight. Turn dough out of pan, and remove waxed paper. Slice dough in half, forming two 8- x 4-inch rectangles. Cut each portion crosswise into ¼-inch slices. Place on ungreased cookie sheets. Bake at 400° for 10 minutes or until lightly browned. Remove to wire racks to cool. Yield: about 5 dozen.

LEMON-NUT REFRIGERATOR COOKIES

1 cup shortening
½ cup sugar
½ cup firmly packed brown sugar
1 egg
1 tablespoon grated lemon rind
2 tablespoons fresh lemon juice
2 cups all-purpose flour
¼ teaspoon baking soda
¼ teaspoon salt
1 cup finely chopped walnuts

Cream shortening in a large mixing bowl; gradually add sugar, beating until light and fluffy. Add egg, lemon rind, and juice, beating well.

Sift together flour, soda, and salt in a medium mixing bowl; gradually add to creamed mixture, mixing until well blended. Stir in walnuts.

Shape dough into 3 rolls, 1½ inches in diameter. Wrap each roll in waxed paper, and chill until firm. Remove waxed paper, and cut into ¼-inch slices. Place 2 inches apart on ungreased cookie sheets. Bake at 400° for 8 to 10 minutes or until lightly browned. Remove to wire racks to cool. Yield: 5½ dozen.

ORANGE-COCONUT REFRIGERATOR COOKIES

1 cup butter or margarine
½ cup sugar
½ cup firmly packed brown sugar
1 egg, lightly beaten
1 teaspoon vanilla extract
1½ cups flaked coconut
3 tablespoons grated orange rind
¼ cup plus 1 tablespoon orange juice
3 cups all-purpose flour
½ teaspoon baking soda

Cream butter in a large mixing bowl; gradually add sugar, beating until light and fluffy. Add egg; beat well. Stir in vanilla, coconut, orange rind, and juice, blending well.

Sift together flour and soda in a medium mixing bowl; add to creamed mixture, blending well.

Shape dough into 2 rolls, 1½ inches in diameter; wrap in waxed paper. Place in freezer until firm. Remove waxed paper, and cut into ¼-inch slices. Place 1-inch apart on ungreased cookie sheets, and bake at 375° for 8 to 10 minutes or until lightly browned. Store in airtight containers. Remove to wire racks to cool. Yield: about 7 dozen.

ORANGE-SPICE COOKIES

1 cup butter or margarine
1½ cups sugar
1 egg
2 tablespoons corn syrup
3 cups all-purpose flour
2 teaspoons baking soda
2 teaspoons ground ginger
2 teaspoons ground cinnamon
½ teaspoon ground cloves
1 tablespoon grated orange rind

Cream butter; gradually add sugar, beating until light and fluffy. Add egg and syrup, beating until well blended. Combine flour, soda, and spices. Add to creamed mixture; mix well. Stir in orange rind.

Shape dough into 2 rolls, 1 inch in diameter. Wrap in waxed paper; chill overnight. Remove waxed paper, and cut into ⅛-inch slices. Place 2 inches apart on ungreased cookie sheets. Bake at 400° for 5 to 6 minutes. Remove to wire racks. Yield: about 8 dozen.

ORANGE-PECAN COOKIES

1 cup shortening
½ cup sugar
½ cup firmly packed brown sugar
1 egg, beaten
2 tablespoons grated orange rind
2 tablespoons orange juice
2 cups all-purpose flour
¼ teaspoon baking soda
½ cup chopped pecans

Cream shortening; gradually add sugar, beating until light and fluffy. Add egg, orange rind, and juice; beat well.

Sift together flour and soda; add to creamed mixture, mixing until well blended. Stir in pecans.

Shape dough into a roll, 2 inches in diameter; cover and chill several hours or overnight. Cut into ⅛-inch slices. Place 2 inches apart on ungreased cookie sheets. Bake at 375° for 10 to 12 minutes. Remove to wire racks to cool. Yield: about 4 dozen.

PEANUT BUTTER REFRIGERATOR COOKIES

½ cup butter or margarine,
   softened
1 cup chunky peanut butter
¾ cup sugar
½ cup firmly packed brown sugar
1 egg, lightly beaten
1 teaspoon vanilla extract
1¼ cups all-purpose flour
1½ teaspoons baking powder
¼ teaspoon salt

Cream butter and peanut butter; add sugar, beating until light and fluffy. Add egg; beat well. Stir in vanilla.

Combine flour, baking powder, and salt. Add to creamed mixture; mix well.

Shape dough into a roll, 2 inches in diameter. Wrap in waxed paper, and chill 3 hours or until firm. Remove waxed paper, and cut into ¼-inch slices. Place 2 inches apart on ungreased cookie sheets. Bake at 350° for 10 minutes or until lightly browned. Remove to wire racks to cool. Yield: about 5 dozen.

PEANUT BUTTER CRUNCHIES

½ cup butter or margarine,
   softened
¾ cup chunky peanut butter
½ cup sugar
½ cup firmly packed brown
   sugar
⅓ cup hot water
2 cups self-rising flour
¼ teaspoon baking soda

Cream butter and peanut butter; gradually add sugar, beating until light and fluffy. Add water, mixing well.

Sift togther flour and soda; Add to creamed mixture, mixing well.

Shape dough into 2 rolls, 2 inches in diameter. Wrap in waxed paper; chill until firm. Remove waxed paper, and cut into ¼-inch slices. Place 2 inches apart on ungreased cookie sheets. Bake at 400° for 8 to 10 minutes. Remove to wire racks to cool. Yield: 4½ dozen.

PECAN PUFFETS

½ cup butter or margarine
1 cup firmly packed brown
   sugar
1 egg
½ teaspoon vanilla extract
2 cups self-rising flour
½ teaspoon cream of tartar
1 cup finely chopped
   pecans

Cream butter in a large mixing bowl; gradually add sugar, beating well. Add egg; beat well. Stir in vanilla.

Sift together flour and cream of tartar in a medium mixing bowl; gradually add to creamed mixture, blending well. Stir in pecans.

Shape dough into 2 rolls, 2-inches in diameter. Wrap in waxed paper, and chill until very firm. Remove waxed paper, and cut into ⅛-inch slices. Place 2 inches apart on ungreased cookie sheets. Bake at 375° for 8 to 10 minutes. Remove to wire racks to cool. Yield: 4 dozen.

GERMAN PECAN COOKIES

3¾ cups finely chopped pecans
3 cups all-purpose flour
2¼ cups sugar
2 teaspoons baking powder
1 tablespoon ground cinnamon
1 teaspoon ground nutmeg
½ teaspoon ground cloves
3 eggs, lightly beaten
¼ cup plus 3 tablespoons butter or
   margarine, melted
1 egg white, lightly beaten

Combine first 7 ingredients; mix well. Add 3 eggs and melted butter; mix well.

Shape dough into two 12-inch-long rolls; wrap in waxed paper, and chill until firm. Remove waxed paper, and cut into ¼-inch slices. Place 1 inch apart on lightly greased cookie sheets; brush tops of cookies with egg white. Bake at 350° for 10 to 12 minutes. Remove to wire racks to cool. Yield: about 6 dozen.

HONEY-PECAN COOKIES

1 egg, lightly beaten
½ cup honey
½ cup butter or margarine,
    softened
½ cup sugar
2 cups all-purpose flour
2 teaspoons baking powder
½ teaspoon salt
1 cup chopped pecans

Combine egg and honey in a small mixing bowl; mix well. Set aside.

Cream butter in a large mixing bowl; gradually add sugar, beating until light and fluffy.

Sift together flour, baking powder, and salt in a medium mixing bowl. Add to creamed mixture, stirring well. Stir in reserved egg mixture and pecans, and mix well.

Shape dough into a roll, 1½ inches in diameter. Wrap in waxed paper, and chill overnight. Remove waxed paper, and cut into ¼-inch slices. Place 2 inches apart on lightly greased cookie sheets. Bake at 375° for 10 to 15 minutes or until lightly browned. Remove to wire racks to cool. Yield: about 5½ dozen.

WHOLE WHEAT-WALNUT COOKIES

½ cup shortening
1 cup sugar
2 eggs, well beaten
1 teaspoon vanilla extract
1¾ cups whole wheat
    flour
¼ teaspoon baking soda
¼ teaspoon salt
½ cup finely chopped black
    walnuts

Cream shortening in a large mixing bowl; gradually add sugar, beating well. Add eggs; beat well. Stir in vanilla.

Combine remaining ingredients, and stir into creamed mixture. Chill dough 2 hours or until firm.

Shape dough into a roll, 2½ inches in diameter; wrap in waxed paper, and chill 3 to 4 hours. Remove waxed paper; cut into ¼-inch slices. Place 2 inches apart on ungreased cookie sheets. Bake at 400° for 6 to 8 minutes. Remove to wire racks to cool. Yield: about 5 dozen.

REFRIGERATOR SANDWICH COOKIES

¾ cup butter
¼ cup sugar
¼ cup firmly packed brown sugar
1 egg yolk
1 teaspoon vanilla extract
1¾ cups all-purpose flour
    Pecan halves
    Vanilla Frosting

Cream butter; gradually add sugar, beating until light and fluffy. Add egg yolk; beat well. Stir in vanilla. Gradually add flour, beating well. Chill slightly.

Shape dough into 2 rolls, 1½ inches in diameter; wrap in waxed paper. Chill overnight. Remove waxed paper, and cut into ⅛-inch slices. Place 2 inches apart on greased cookie sheets. Bake at 350° for 8 to 10 minutes. Remove to wire racks to cool. Spread Vanilla Frosting evenly over bottom sides of half the cookies; top with remaining cookies, bottom sides down, to make sandwiches. Top each with a dollop of frosting and a pecan half. Yield: about 3 dozen.

Vanilla Frosting:

¼ cup butter or margarine
2½ cups sifted powdered
    sugar
1 egg white
½ teaspoon vanilla extract
    Food coloring

Cream butter in a large mixing bowl; add sugar alternately with egg white (at room temperature), beating until light and fluffy. Stir in vanilla. Add food coloring, as desired, stirring well. Yield: frosting for about 3 dozen cookies.

THREE-IN-ONE COOKIES

1 cup butter or margarine
½ cup sugar
½ cup firmly packed brown sugar
1 egg
½ teaspoon vanilla extract
2 cups all-purpose flour
½ teaspoon baking soda
¼ teaspoon salt
½ cup flaked coconut
½ cup chopped raisins
½ cup chopped pecans

Cream butter in a large mixing bowl; gradually add sugar, beating until light and fluffy. Add egg and vanilla; beat until well blended.

Combine flour, soda, and salt in a medium mixing bowl; add to creamed mixture, beating well.

Divide dough into thirds. Add coconut to one portion, raisins to second portion, and pecans to remaining portion; mix well. Shape each portion into a roll, 1-inch in diameter; wrap in waxed paper, and chill overnight.

Remove waxed paper, and cut into ⅛-inch slices. Place 2 inches apart on greased cookie sheets. Bake at 375° for 8 minutes or until lightly browned. Remove to wire racks to cool. Yield: 6 dozen.

RIBBON COOKIES

1 cup butter or margarine
1½ cups sugar
1 egg, beaten
1 teaspoon vanilla extract
2½ cups all-purpose flour
1½ teaspoons baking powder
½ teaspoon salt
¼ cup chopped candied cherries
¼ cup chopped pecans
1 (1-ounce) square unsweetened chocolate, melted
2 tablespoons poppyseeds

Line bottom and sides of a 9- x 5- x 3-inch loafpan with waxed paper, and set aside.

Cream butter in a large mixing bowl; gradually add sugar, beating until light and fluffy. Add egg; beat well. Stir in vanilla.

Sift together flour, baking powder, and salt in a medium mixing bowl. Add to creamed mixture; mix well.

Divide dough into thirds. Add cherries to one portion, and spread evenly in prepared pan. Add pecans and melted chocolate to second portion; spread evenly over dough in pan. Add poppyseeds to remaining portion; spread evenly over dough in pan. Cover with waxed paper; chill overnight.

Turn dough out of pan, and remove waxed paper; cut into ⅛-inch slices. Place 2 inches apart on greased cookie sheets. Bake at 400° for 10 minutes. Remove to wire racks to cool. Yield: 6 to 8 dozen.

NEOPOLITAN COOKIES

1 cup butter or margarine, softened
1½ cups sugar
1 egg
1 teaspoon vanilla extract
2½ cups all-purpose flour
1½ teaspoons baking powder
½ teaspoon salt
½ teaspoon almond extract
Red food coloring
½ cup chopped pecans or walnuts
1 (1-ounce) square unsweetened chocolate, melted

Line bottom and sides of a 9- x 5- x 3-inch loafpan with waxed paper.

Cream butter in a large mixing bowl; gradually add sugar, beating until light and fluffy. Add egg; beat well. Stir in vanilla.

Combine flour, baking powder, and salt in a medium mixing bowl; add to creamed mixture, beating just until blended.

Divide dough into thirds. Add almond extract and 5 drops red food coloring to one portion; spread mixture evenly in prepared pan. Add pecans to second portion; spread mixture evenly over dough in pan. Add melted chocolate to remaining portion; spread mixture evenly over dough in pan. Cover and refrigerate overnight.

Turn dough out of pan, and remove waxed paper. Cut dough in half lengthwise; cut each half crosswise into ⅛-inch slices. Place 1 inch apart on ungreased cookie sheets. Bake at 350° for 10 to 12 minutes. Remove to wire racks to cool. Store in airtight containers. Yield: 5 dozen.

SLICE-OF-FRUIT REFRIGERATOR COOKIES

    1 cup shortening
 1½ cups sugar
    2 eggs
    1 teaspoon vanilla extract
    3 tablespoons lemon juice
  ¼ cup plus 3 tablespoons orange
        juice
 4½ cups all-purpose
        flour
  ½ teaspoon salt
        Yellow, orange, and green paste
        food coloring
 1½ teaspoons grated lemon
        rind
 1½ teaspoons grated orange rind
 1½ teaspoons grated lime rind
        Yellow, orange, and green
        colored sugar
        Royal Icing

Cream shortening in a large mixing bowl; gradually add sugar, beating until light and fluffy. Add eggs; beat well. Stir in vanilla and juices.

Combine flour and salt in a medium mixing bowl; gradually add to creamed mixture, mixing until well blended. (Mixture will be stiff.)

Divide dough into fourths. Add desired amount of yellow food coloring and lemon rind to one portion, mixing well; add desired amount of orange food coloring and orange rind to second portion, mixing well. Add desired amount of green food coloring and lime rind to third portion, mixing well. Leave remaining portion plain.

Shape each portion of colored dough into a 6-inch-long roll. Divide plain dough into thirds; roll each portion into a 6-inch square. Wrap a square around each roll of colored dough, pressing lightly to combine dough. Roll each in matching colored sugar. (To make colored sugar, stir a small amount of liquid food coloring into sugar, blending until desired color is reached.) Wrap in waxed paper and refrigerate several hours or overnight.

Remove waxed paper, and cut rolls into ¼-inch slices; cut each slice in half. Place 1 inch apart on ungreased cookie sheets. Bake at 400° for 6 to 8 minutes. Remove to wire racks to cool.

Spoon Royal Icing into a pastry bag fitted with a No. 3 round tip. Pipe designs on cookies to resemble fruit sections. Let dry thoroughly. Yield: 6½ dozen.

Royal Icing:

    1 egg white
  ⅛ teaspoon cream of tartar
    1 cup plus 3 tablespoons sifted
        powdered sugar

Combine egg white (at room temperature) and cream of tartar in a medium mixing bowl. Beat at medium speed of an electric mixer until foamy. Gradually add sugar, 2 tablespoons at a time, beating at high speed 5 minutes or until stiff peaks form. Yield: icing for 6½ dozen cookies.

Note: Royal Icing dries very quickly; keep covered at all times with plastic wrap. Food coloring may be added to icing, if desired.

PEPPERMINT SPIRALS

1 cup butter or margarine,
    softened
1½ cups sugar
1 egg
1 teaspoon peppermint extract
2½ cups all-purpose flour
1½ teaspoons baking powder
½ teaspoon salt
    Red food coloring

Cream butter; gradually add sugar, beating until light and fluffy. Add egg and peppermint extract; beat well.

Combine flour, baking powder, and salt; add to creamed mixture, beating just until blended.

Divide dough in half; tint one portion with desired amount of red food coloring. Cover and chill both portions.

On sheets of floured waxed paper, roll each portion to a 16- x 8-inch rectangle. Invert plain dough directly on top of red dough; remove waxed paper from plain dough. Roll up jellyroll fashion, beginning with long side; remove remaining waxed paper while rolling. Cover and refrigerate overnight. Cut into ¼-inch slices, and place 2 inches apart on ungreased cookie sheets. Bake at 350° for 10 to 12 minutes. Remove to wire racks to cool. Yield: about 5 dozen.

CHOCOLATE PINWHEELS

½ cup butter or margarine,
    softened
½ cup sugar
3 tablespoons milk
1 egg yolk, beaten
½ teaspoon vanilla extract
1½ cups all-purpose flour
1½ teaspoons baking powder
⅛ teaspoon salt
1 (1-ounce) square unsweetened
    chocolate, melted

Cream butter; gradually add sugar, beating until light and fluffy. Add milk, egg yolk, and vanilla, stirring well.

Sift together flour, baking powder, and salt; add to creamed mixture, stirring until well blended.

Divide dough in half. Add chocolate to one portion; mix well, and chill. Roll remaining dough to a 14- x 6-inch rectangle on waxed paper. Repeat procedure with chocolate dough. Invert chocolate rectangle directly on top of light rectangle; remove waxed paper from chocolate dough. Roll up jellyroll fashion, beginning with long side; remove remaining waxed paper while rolling. Chill 1 hour. Cut into ¼-inch slices; place 2 inches apart on greased cookie sheets. Bake at 375° for 8 to 10 minutes. Cool slightly on cookie sheets, and remove to wire racks. Yield: about 5 dozen.

DATE PINWHEELS

1 (8-ounce) package pitted dates
½ cup water
¼ cup sugar
½ cup butter or margarine,
    softened
1 cup firmly packed brown sugar
1 egg
2 cups all-purpose flour
½ teaspoon baking soda
¼ teaspoon salt
½ teaspoon ground cinnamon

Combine dates, water, and ¼ cup sugar in a medium saucepan. Bring to a boil. Reduce heat, and simmer 5 minutes, stirring constantly. Let cool.

Cream butter; gradually add brown sugar, beating well. Add egg; beat well.

Combine flour, soda, salt, and cinnamon; add to creamed mixture, stirring well. Cover and chill at least 1 hour.

Roll dough to a 16- x 10-inch rectangle on waxed paper; spread with date filling. Roll up jellyroll fashion, beginning with long end; remove waxed paper while rolling. Pinch ends to seal. Cover; chill overnight. Cut into ¼-inch slices; place 2 inches apart on ungreased cookie sheets. Bake at 375° for 8 minutes or until lightly browned. Remove to wire racks. Yield: about 4½ dozen.

DATE-NUT PINWHEELS

1 (8-ounce) package pitted dates,
   chopped
1 cup sugar
1 cup hot water
1 cup finely chopped walnuts
1 cup butter or margarine,
   softened
2 cups firmly packed brown
   sugar
2 eggs
1 teaspoon vanilla extract
3½ cups all-purpose flour
½ teaspoon baking soda
½ teaspoon cream of tartar
½ teaspoon salt

Combine dates, sugar, and water in a medium saucepan; cook over medium heat, stirring constantly, about 6 to 8 minutes or until mixture thickens. Remove from heat; stir in walnuts. Let cool completely.

Cream butter in a large mixing bowl; gradually add brown sugar, beating well. Add eggs; beat well. Stir in vanilla.

Combine flour, soda, cream of tartar, and salt in a medium mixing bowl; add to creamed mixture, stirring well.

Divide dough into thirds. Roll each portion into a 12-inch square on separate sheets of waxed paper; spread each square with one-third of reserved date mixture. Lifting up edge of waxed paper, gently peel off dough, and roll up jellyroll fashion, beginning with long end. Wrap rolls in waxed paper, and chill overnight. Remove waxed paper. Cut into ¼-inch slices, and place 2 inches apart on greased cookie sheets. Bake at 350° for 8 to 10 minutes. Remove to wire racks to cool. Store in airtight containers. Yield: about 6 dozen.

BUTTERSCOTCH PINWHEELS

½ cup shortening, divided
¼ cup firmly packed brown sugar
1 egg
¾ cup butterscotch morsels,
   melted
1 teaspoon vanilla extract, divided
2 cups all-purpose flour, divided
¼ teaspoon baking soda
½ teaspoon salt, divided
½ cup sugar
1 egg
¼ teaspoon baking powder
1 (1-ounce) square unsweetened
   chocolate, melted

Cream ¼ cup shortening in a medium mixing bowl; gradually add brown sugar, beating until light and fluffy. Add 1 egg, beating well. Stir in melted butterscotch morsels and ½ teaspoon vanilla, blending well.

Sift together 1 cup flour, soda, and ¼ teaspoon salt; add to creamed mixture, stirring until well blended.

Roll dough to a 10- x 7-inch rectangle between 2 sheets of waxed paper.

Repeat procedure with remaining ingredients, substituting ½ cup sugar for brown sugar, baking powder for soda, and chocolate for butterscotch.

Remove waxed paper from tops of dough; invert chocolate rectangle directly on top of butterscotch rectangle. Remove waxed paper from chocolate dough. Roll up jellyroll fashion, beginning with long side; remove remaining waxed paper while rolling. Cover and chill 1 hour. Cut into ¼-inch slices; place 2 inches apart on lightly greased cookie sheets. Bake at 375° for 6 minutes or until lightly browned. Remove to wire racks. Yield: about 5½ dozen.

SHAPED COOKIES

BOURBON BALLS

2 tablespoons cocoa
1 cup sifted powdered sugar
¼ cup bourbon
2 tablespoons light corn syrup
2 cups crushed vanilla wafers
1 cup finely chopped pecans
  Additional sifted powdered sugar

Sift together cocoa and 1 cup sugar. Combine bourbon and syrup; add to cocoa mixture, and stir well. Add wafer crumbs and pecans; mix well.

Shape into ¾-inch balls, and roll in additional sugar to coat. Allow to dry before serving. Yield: 3 dozen.

DATE-NUT BALLS

½ cup butter or margarine
¾ cup sugar
1 (8-ounce) package pitted dates, chopped
2½ cups crisp rice cereal
1 cup chopped pecans
  Flaked coconut (optional)
  Sifted powdered sugar (optional)

Combine butter, sugar, and dates in a medium saucepan. Bring to a boil; cook, stirring constantly, 3 minutes. Stir in cereal and pecans; cool to touch. Shape into 1-inch balls, and roll in coconut or powdered sugar, if desired. Store in airtight containers. Yield: about 4 dozen.

ORANGE BALLS

1 (12-ounce) package vanilla wafers
1 (16-ounce) package powdered sugar, sifted
½ cup butter or margarine, softened
1 (6-ounce) can concentrated frozen orange juice, thawed and undiluted
1 cup finely chopped pecans
  Flaked coconut (optional)

Crush vanilla wafers to make fine crumbs. Add sugar, butter, and orange juice concentrate, mixing well.

Shape dough into 1-inch balls. Roll balls in pecans or coconut, if desired; chill until firm. Yield: 6 dozen.

CRÈME DE CACAO BALLS

2½ cups crushed chocolate sandwich cookies
1 cup chopped walnuts
1 cup sifted powdered sugar
⅓ cup crème de cacao
2 tablespoons dark corn syrup
  Additional sifted powdered sugar

Combine crushed cookies, walnuts, and 1 cup sugar. Add crème de cacao and syrup; mix well. Shape dough into 1-inch balls; roll in additional powdered sugar. Place in an airtight container; chill overnight. Yield: 3 dozen.

SHORTBREAD COOKIES

1 **cup butter, softened**
½ **cup sifted powdered sugar**
1 **cup all-purpose flour**
½ **cup cornstarch**

Cream butter; gradually add sugar, beating until light and fluffy.

Sift together flour and cornstarch in a medium mixing bowl; add to creamed mixture, blending well. Shape dough into a ball, and chill 1 to 2 hours.

Shape dough into 1-inch balls, and place 3 inches apart on ungreased cookie sheets. Gently flatten cookies to ½-inch thickness, using a fork dipped in flour. Bake at 300° for 20 to 22 minutes. Cool slightly on cookie sheets; remove to wire racks to cool completely. Yield: 4 dozen.

HIGHLAND SHORTBREAD

2 **cups butter**
1 **cup sugar**
4 **cups all-purpose flour**
½ **teaspoon salt**
   Pecan halves
   Sifted powdered sugar

Cream butter; gradually add 1 cup sugar, beating until light and fluffy.

Sift together flour and salt; add to creamed mixture. (Add more flour, if needed, to make dough easy to handle.)

Shape dough into ¾-inch balls; place 2 inches apart on greased cookie sheets. Gently press a pecan half in center of each. Bake at 350° for 8 to 10 minutes or until lightly browned. Roll in powdered sugar while warm. Yield: 6 dozen.

SHORTBREAD FANS

1 **cup butter, softened**
½ **cup sugar**
2½ **cups all-purpose flour**

Cream butter in a medium mixing bowl; gradually add sugar, beating until light and fluffy. Add flour, stirring until thoroughly blended.

Divide dough into fourths; place each portion on a lightly greased cookie sheet, and pat each evenly into a 5-inch circle. Score the surface of each circle into 8 wedges, using a wooden pick. Press around outer edge of each circle with tines of a fork. Bake at 325° for 25 minutes or until lightly browned. Remove from oven; make deep indentations along scored lines. Remove to wire racks to cool. Break into wedges to serve. Store in airtight containers. Yield: about 2½ dozen.

Note: Chilled dough may be pressed into a floured shortbread mold and turned out onto a lightly greased cookie sheet. Bake as directed.

SAND CRESCENTS

1 **cup butter or margarine**
¼ **cup plus 1 tablespoon sifted**
   powdered sugar
1 **teaspoon vanilla**
   extract
2½ **cups all-purpose flour**
1½ **cups chopped pecans**
   Additional sifted powdered
   sugar

Cream butter in a large mixing bowl; gradually add ¼ cup plus 1 tablespoon sugar, beating until light and fluffy. Stir in vanilla, blending well. Gradually add flour and chopped pecans, mixing just until well blended.

Shape dough into small crescents; place 2 inches apart on ungreased cookie sheets. Bake at 250° for 40 to 50 minutes. Remove to a wire rack to cool completely. Roll in additional powdered sugar. Store in airtight containers. Yield: about 2 dozen.

RUSSIAN TEA CAKES

1 cup butter or margarine
½ cup sifted powdered sugar
1 teaspoon vanilla extract
2¼ cups all-purpose flour
¼ teaspoon salt
¾ cup finely chopped pecans
   Additional sifted powdered sugar

Cream butter in a large mixing bowl; gradually add ½ cup sugar, beating until light and fluffy. Stir in vanilla.

Combine flour, salt, and pecans; gradually add to creamed mixture, blending well. Chill until firm.

Shape dough into 1-inch balls; place 2 inches apart on ungreased cookie sheets. Bake at 400° for 12 to 15 minutes or until edges are lightly browned. Roll in additional powdered sugar while warm. Cool on wire racks, and roll again in powdered sugar. Yield: about 4 dozen.

SNICKERDOODLES

1 tablespoon sugar
1 tablespoon ground cinnamon
1 cup shortening
1½ cups sugar
2 eggs
1 teaspoon vanilla extract
2¾ cups all-purpose flour
1 teaspoon baking soda
½ teaspoon salt
2 teaspoons cream of tartar

Combine 1 tablespoon sugar and cinnamon in a small mixing bowl.

Cream shortening; gradually add 1½ cups sugar, beating well. Add eggs; beat well. Stir in vanilla.

Sift together flour, soda, salt, and cream of tartar in a medium mixing bowl. Add to creamed mixture; mix well.

Shape dough into 1-inch balls, and roll in reserved cinnamon mixture. Place 2 inches apart on lightly greased cookie sheets. Bake at 400° for 6 minutes or until lightly browned. Remove to wire racks to cool. Yield: about 4 dozen.

OLD-FASHIONED SUGAR 'N SPICE COOKIES

½ cup butter, softened
¾ cup sugar
¾ cup firmly packed brown sugar
2 eggs
   Juice of 1 lemon
1 teaspoon vanilla extract
3 cups all-purpose flour
½ teaspoon baking soda
½ teaspoon ground cinnamon
¼ teaspoon ground allspice

Cream butter in a large mixing bowl; gradually add sugar, beating well. Add eggs; beat well. Stir in lemon juice and vanilla.

Sift together flour, soda, cinnamon, and allspice in a medium mixing bowl; gradually add to creamed mixture, stirring well.

Press dough from a cookie press 2 inches apart onto lightly greased cookie sheets, making 12-inch ribbon-like strips. Bake at 350° for 8 minutes or until edges are lightly browned. Cut each strip into 3-inch segments while warm. Carefully remove from cookie sheets, and cool on wire racks. Yield: about 9 dozen.

SWEDISH MELTING MOMENTS

1 cup butter or margarine
¼ cup plus 1½ tablespoons sifted powdered sugar
1¼ cups all-purpose flour
½ cup cornstarch
¼ teaspoon almond extract
¼ teaspoon orange extract
   Cookie Glaze

Cream butter in a large mixing bowl; gradually add sugar, beating until light and fluffy. Sift in flour and cornstarch; mix well. Add flavorings, blending well; chill 1 hour.

Shape dough into 1-inch balls, and place 3 inches apart on greased cookie sheets. Flatten each with bottom of a small glass dipped in water. Bake at 350° for 10 minutes. (Cookies do not brown.) Carefully remove to a wire rack; spread Cookie Glaze evenly over each cookie while warm. Let cool, and store in airtight containers. Yield: 2 dozen.

Cookie Glaze:

   1 cup sifted powdered
      sugar
   1 tablespoon butter, melted
   1 tablespoon lemon juice
   1 tablespoon orange juice

Combine all ingredients; beat with a wire whisk until smooth. Yield: glaze for 2 dozen cookies.

NEW ENGLAND GINGERSNAPS

   ¾ cup butter or margarine
   1 cup sugar
   1 egg
   ¼ cup molasses
   2 cups all-purpose flour
   2 teaspoons baking soda
   1 teaspoon ground ginger
   1 teaspoon ground cinnamon
   1 teaspoon ground cloves
      Additional sugar

Cream butter in a large mixing bowl; gradually add 1 cup sugar, beating until light and fluffy. Add egg and molasses, and beat well.

Sift together flour, soda, and spices. Add to creamed mixture, beating until smooth. Chill 2 hours.

Shape dough into ¾-inch balls, and roll in additional sugar to coat well. Place 2 inches apart on greased baking sheets. Bake at 350° for 11 to 12 minutes. (Cookies will puff up and then flatten.) Cool slightly on cookie sheets; remove to wire racks to cool completely. Yield: about 6 dozen.

GINGER COOKIES

   ¾ cup shortening
   1 cup sugar
   1 egg
   ¼ cup molasses
   2 cups all-purpose flour
   2 teaspoons baking soda
   ½ teaspoon salt
   1 tablespoon ground ginger
   1 teaspoon ground cinnamon
      Additional sugar

Cream shortening; gradually add 1 cup sugar, beating until light and fluffy. Add egg and molasses; beat well.

Combine flour, soda, salt, ginger, and cinnamon in a medium mixing bowl; add to creamed mixture, mixing well.

Shape dough into 1-inch balls, and roll in additional sugar. Place 2 inches apart on ungreased cookie sheets. Bake at 350° for 8 to 10 minutes. Cool on cookie sheets 5 minutes; remove to wire racks, using a spatula, and cool completely. Yield: 7 dozen.

ALMOND FINGERS

   1 cup butter, softened
   ½ cup sifted powdered sugar
   1½ cups all-purpose flour
      Dash of salt
   1 teaspoon almond extract
   2 cups chopped toasted almonds
      Additional sifted powdered sugar

Cream butter; gradually add ½ cup sugar, beating until light and fluffy.

Sift together flour and salt; add to creamed mixture; blend well. Add almond extract and almonds; beat well. Chill 30 minutes.

Shape dough into 2-inch rolls, using 1 tablespoon dough for each roll. Place 2 inches apart on lightly greased cookie sheets. Bake at 325° for 20 minutes or until lightly browned.

Roll warm cookies in additional sugar, and sprinkle excess over tops. Cool on wire racks. Store in airtight containers. Yield: 6 dozen.

CHINESE ALMOND COOKIES

1 cup butter or margarine
1 cup sugar
1 egg
1 teaspoon almond
    extract
2½ cups all-purpose flour
1 teaspoon baking powder
½ teaspoon salt
1 tablespoon water
    Whole blanched almonds

Cream butter in a large mixing bowl; gradually add sugar, beating until light and fluffy. Add egg, beating well. Stir in almond extract.

Sift together flour, baking powder, and salt in a medium mixing bowl; add to creamed mixture alternately with water, beginning and ending with flour mixture. Chill 2 hours.

Shape dough into 1-inch balls; place 2 inches apart on ungreased baking sheets, and press each ball to ¼-inch thickness with bottom of a small glass. Press an almond into center of each. Bake at 350° for 12 to 15 minutes. Remove to wire racks to cool. Yield: about 5 dozen.

TOASTED ALMOND FINGERS

1 cup butter or margarine,
    softened
¾ cup sifted powdered sugar
1 tablespoon milk
1 teaspoon vanilla extract
2 cups all-purpose flour
¼ teaspoon salt
2 cups finely chopped toasted
    almonds
1 (6-ounce) package semisweet
    chocolate morsels
1 tablespoon shortening

Cream butter in a large mixing bowl; gradually add sugar, beating until light and fluffy. Add milk and vanilla, beating well. Add flour and salt, mixing until well blended. Stir in almonds. Chill dough thoroughly.

Shape dough into 2-inch rolls, using 1 tablespoon dough for each; place 2 inches apart on ungreased cookie sheets. Bake at 325° for 15 to 17 minutes or until lightly browned. Cool on wire racks.

Melt chocolate and shortening in top of a double boiler over simmering water. Dip one end of each cookie in chocolate, letting excess drip off; leave cookies on wire racks until chocolate is set. Yield: about 4 dozen.

ALMOND-OATMEAL COOKIES

⅓ cup shortening
½ cup sugar
1½ cups quick-cooking or regular
    oats, uncooked
½ teaspoon vanilla
    extract
¼ cup water
¾ cup all-purpose flour
1 teaspoon baking powder
½ teaspoon salt
½ cup toasted diced almonds

Cream shortening in a large mixing bowl; gradually add sugar, beating until light and fluffy. Add oats, blending well. Stir in vanilla and water.

Sift together flour, baking powder, and salt in a medium mixing bowl; add to creamed mixture, stirring well. Stir in almonds. Chill 1 hour or until firm.

Shape dough into ¾-inch balls; place 2 inches apart on greased cookie sheets, and flatten with bottom of a glass dipped in flour. Bake at 400° for 8 to 10 minutes. Remove to wire racks to cool. Yield: about 3 dozen.

ORANGE-OATMEAL COOKIES

2 cups Basic Cookie Mix
1 egg, lightly beaten
2 to 3 teaspoons grated orange
    rind
1 tablespoon plus 1 teaspoon
    orange juice
½ cup chopped pecans or walnuts

Combine all ingredients, mixing well. Shape dough into 1-inch balls; place 2 inches apart on ungreased cookie sheets. Bake at 375° for 10 to 12 minutes. Remove to wire racks to cool. Yield: about 2½ dozen.

Note: Lemon rind and juice or spices may be substituted for orange rind and juice.

Basic Cookie Mix:

1 cup shortening
1 cup sugar
1 cup firmly packed brown sugar
2 cups all-purpose flour
1 teaspoon baking powder
1 teaspoon baking soda
¼ teaspoon salt
1 teaspoon ground cinnamon
2 cups quick-cooking oats, uncooked
2 cups corn flakes

Combine shortening and sugar in a large bowl, blending well.

Combine remaining ingredients; mix well. Add to sugar mixture, blending well. Cover and store in refrigerator until ready to use. Yield: cookie mix for about 10 dozen cookies.

OATMEAL CRINKLES

1¼ cups sugar, divided
1 teaspoon ground cinnamon
1 cup shortening
1 cup firmly packed brown sugar
2 eggs
1 teaspoon vanilla extract
¼ teaspoon almond extract
2 cups all-purpose flour
1 teaspoon baking powder
1 teaspoon baking soda
1 teaspoon salt
2½ cups regular oats, uncooked
1½ cups raisins

Combine ¼ cup sugar and cinnamon in a small mixing bowl; stir until well blended, and set aside.

Cream shortening in a large mixing bowl; add remaining 1 cup sugar, brown sugar, eggs, and flavorings, beating until well blended.

Combine flour, baking powder, soda, and salt in a medium mixing bowl; add oats and raisins, stirring well. Add to creamed mixture, mixing well.

Shape dough into 1-inch balls; roll in reserved cinnamon mixture, and place 2 inches apart on greased cookie sheets. Bake at 350° for 10 minutes. Cool slightly on cookie sheets; remove to wire racks to cool completely. Yield: about 5 dozen.

OATMEAL-DATE COOKIES

1 cup butter or margarine
⅔ cup sugar
1 cup firmly packed brown sugar
1 egg, beaten
1 teaspoon vanilla extract
2½ cups all-purpose flour
2 teaspoons baking soda
⅛ teaspoon salt
1 cup regular oats, uncooked
1 cup chopped dates
1 cup chopped pecans
Additional sugar

Cream butter in a large mixing bowl; gradually add ⅔ cup sugar and brown sugar, beating until light and fluffy. Add egg; beat well. Stir in vanilla.

Sift together flour, soda, and salt; add to creamed mixture, blending well. Stir in oats, dates, and pecans.

Shape dough into ¾-inch balls, and roll in additional sugar. Place 2 inches apart on greased cookie sheets. Bake at 350° for 10 to 12 minutes. (Cookies will puff up and then flatten.) Remove to wire racks to cool. Store in airtight containers. Yield: about 7 dozen.

BUTTERSCOTCH COOKIES

¾ cup shortening
¾ cup sugar
½ cup molasses
1 egg
2¼ cups all-purpose flour
1½ teaspoons baking
    soda
½ teaspoon salt
1 teaspoon ground cinnamon
½ teaspoon ground ginger
1 (6-ounce) package butterscotch
    morsels
    Additional sugar
    Pecan halves

Cream shortening in a large mixing bowl; gradually add ¾ cup sugar, beating until light and fluffy. Add molasses and egg; beat well.

Combine flour, soda, salt, cinnamon, and ginger. Add to creamed mixture, beating well. Stir in butterscotch morsels. Cover and refrigerate at least 2 hours.

Shape dough into 1-inch balls; roll in additional sugar to coat well. Place balls 2 inches apart on greased cookie sheets. Gently press a pecan half in center of each ball.

Bake at 350° for 10 minutes or until browned. Remove to wire racks to cool. Yield: about 5 dozen.

CHUNKS O' CHOCOLATE COOKIES

1 cup shortening
¾ cup sugar
¾ cup firmly packed brown
    sugar
3 eggs
1 teaspoon vanilla extract
3 cups all-purpose flour
1 teaspoon baking soda
¼ teaspoon salt
½ cup chopped pecans
1 cup chopped dates
1 (4-ounce) package sweet baking
    chocolate

Cream shortening in a large mixing bowl; gradually add sugar, beating until light and fluffy. Add eggs; beat well. Stir in vanilla.

Sift together flour, soda, and salt in a medium mixing bowl; stir in pecans to coat well. Add to creamed mixture, blending well; stir in dates. Break chocolate into raisin-size pieces, and add to mixture, stirring well. Chill 8 hours or overnight.

Shape dough into 1½-inch balls; place 2 inches apart on ungreased cookie sheets. Gently flatten balls with a fork dipped in flour. Bake at 400° for 8 to 10 minutes. Remove from cookie sheets immediately, and cool completely on wire racks. Store in airtight containers. Yield: about 7 dozen.

DEVIL'S FOOD COOKIES

½ cup shortening
1 cup sugar
2 eggs
1¾ cups all-purpose flour
½ cup cocoa
1 teaspoon baking soda
½ teaspoon salt
1 teaspoon vanilla extract
1 teaspoon butter flavoring
    About 20 large marshmallows,
    cut in half
    Chocolate Frosting

Cream shortening in a large mixing bowl; gradually add sugar, beating until well blended. Add eggs, one at a time, beating well.

Sift together flour, soda, salt, and cocoa in a medium mixing bowl; add to creamed mixture, beating until well blended. Stir in flavorings, blending well. (Dough will be stiff.) Cover and chill at least 30 minutes.

Shape dough into 1-inch balls; place 2 inches apart on greased cookie sheets.

Bake at 350° for 8 minutes. Place a marshmallow half on top of each cookie; bake an additional 2 minutes. Remove to wire racks, and spread Chocolate Frosting evenly over each cookie. Leave cookies on wire racks until frosting is set. Store in airtight containers. Yield: about 3½ dozen.

Chocolate Frosting:

½ cup semisweet chocolate
    morsels
¼ cup milk
2 tablespoons butter or
    margarine
2 cups sifted powdered sugar

Combine chocolate morsels, milk, and butter in medium saucepan; cook over low heat, stirring constantly, until chocolate melts. Add sugar, beating until mixture is smooth. (Additional milk may be added to yield desired spreading consistency.) Yield: frosting for about 3½ dozen cookies.

CHOCOLATE DROPS

2 (1-ounce) squares unsweetened
    chocolate
½ cup shortening
1⅔ cups firmly packed brown
    sugar
2 eggs
1 teaspoon vanilla extract
2 cups all-purpose flour
2 teaspoons baking powder
¾ teaspoon salt
1 teaspoon ground cinnamon
⅓ cup milk
⅔ cup chopped pecans
    Sifted powdered sugar

Melt chocolate in top of a double boiler over simmering water. Remove from heat, and set aside to cool.

Cream shortening; gradually add brown sugar, beating well. Add eggs; beat well. Stir in chocolate and vanilla.

Combine flour, baking powder, salt, and cinnamon in a medium mixing bowl; add to creamed mixture alternately with milk, beginning and ending with flour mixture. Stir in pecans. Cover and chill at least 2 hours.

Coat hands with powdered sugar. Shape dough into 1-inch balls, and roll in powdered sugar to coat well. Place 2 inches apart on greased cookie sheets; chill 30 minutes. Bake at 350° for 20 minutes. Remove to wire racks to cool. Yield: 5 dozen.

MINT CHOCOLATE SNAPS

1 (6-ounce) package semisweet
    chocolate morsels
½ cup plus 1½ tablespoons
    shortening
¾ cup sugar
1 egg
¼ cup light corn syrup
1 teaspoon peppermint extract
1 teaspoon vanilla extract
2 cups all-purpose flour
1 teaspoon baking soda
¼ teaspoon salt
¼ cup crushed peppermint
    candy
    Additional sugar

Melt chocolate morsels in top of a double boiler over simmering water.

Cream shortening in a large mixing bowl; gradually add ¾ cup sugar, beating until light and fluffy. Add chocolate, beating well. Add egg, syrup, and flavorings; beat well.

Combine flour, soda, and salt in a large mixing bowl; stir in chocolate mixture and peppermint candy.

Shape dough into 1-inch balls, and roll in additional sugar; place 2 inches apart on ungreased cookie sheets. Bake at 350° for 12 to 15 minutes. Cool on cookie sheets 5 minutes; remove to wire racks. Store in airtight containers. Yield: about 7 dozen.

CHERRY BONBONS

1 cup butter or margarine,
    softened
1½ cups sifted powdered sugar
1 tablespoon plus 1½ teaspoons
    vanilla extract
2¾ cups all-purpose flour
¼ teaspoon salt
1 tablespoon milk
2 (8-ounce) jars maraschino
    cherries, drained
    Rainbow Glaze
    Chocolate Glaze
    Chopped walnuts

Cream butter in a large mixing bowl; gradually add sugar, beating until light and fluffy. Stir in vanilla. Add flour, salt, and milk, blending well. Shape dough around each cherry, using 1 tablespoon dough at a time; place 1 inch apart on ungreased cookie sheets. Bake at 350° for 12 to 15 minutes. Remove to wire racks to cool.

Dip tops of cookies in Rainbow Glaze or Chocolate Glaze; sprinkle immediately with walnuts. Yield: about 3 dozen.

Rainbow Glaze:

2½ cups sifted powdered sugar
3 to 4 tablespoons water
    Yellow, pink, and green food
    coloring

Combine sugar and water; beat until smooth. Divide glaze into thirds in small mixing bowls. Stir in food coloring using a different color in each bowl. Yield: glaze for about 2 dozen cookies.

Chocolate Glaze:

1 cup sifted powdered sugar
2 to 3 tablespoons water
1 (1-ounce) square unsweetened
    chocolate, melted
1 teaspoon vanilla extract

Combine all ingredients in a medium mixing bowl; beat with a wire whisk until smooth. Yield: glaze for about 1 dozen cookies.

CHERRY DELIGHTS

1 cup butter or margarine,
    softened
½ cup sugar
½ cup light corn syrup
2 eggs, separated
2½ cups all-purpose flour
2 cups finely chopped pecans
    Candied cherry halves

Cream butter in a large mixing bowl; gradually add sugar, beating until light and fluffy. Add syrup, egg yolks, and flour; mix well. Chill.

Shape dough into 1-inch balls; dip each in lightly beaten egg whites, and roll in pecans. Gently press a cherry half, cut side down, into center of each. Place 1½ inches apart on greased cookie sheets. Bake at 325° for 20 minutes. Remove to wire racks. Yield: 4 dozen.

CHERRY-PECAN BALLS

1 cup shortening
1 (3-ounce) package cream cheese,
    softened
1 cup sugar
1 egg
1 teaspoon almond extract
2½ cups all-purpose flour
¼ teaspoon baking soda
½ teaspoon salt
1¾ cups finely chopped pecans
36 marachino cherries, halved

Cream shortening and cream cheese in a large mixing bowl; gradually add sugar, beating until light and fluffy. Add egg; beat well. Stir in almond extract.

Sift together flour, soda, and salt in a medium mixing bowl; add to creamed mixture, beating well. Chill 1 hour.

Shape dough into 1-inch balls; roll in pecans. Place 2 inches apart on ungreased cookie sheets. Gently press a cherry half in center of each cookie. Bake at 350° for 12 to 15 minutes. Remove to wire racks to cool. Store in airtight containers in refrigerator up to 1 week. Yield: 6 dozen.

COCONUT BALLS

1 cup butter or margarine,
   softened
¼ cup sifted powdered sugar
1 tablespoon water
2 teaspoons vanilla extract
2 cups all-purpose flour
1 cup chopped pecans
   Frosting (recipe follows)
1 (8-ounce) package shredded
   coconut

Cream butter in a large mixing bowl; gradually add sugar, beating until light and fluffy. Stir in water and vanilla. Add flour, mixing well. Stir in pecans.

Shape dough into 1-inch balls; place 2 inches apart on ungreased cookie sheets. Bake at 300° for 20 minutes or until lightly browned. Cool on cookie sheets. Dip cookies in frosting, and roll in coconut. Yield: about 4 dozen.

Frosting:

1 (16-ounce) package powdered
   sugar, sifted
½ cup milk or half-and-half
½ teaspoon vanilla or almond
   extract
   Dash of salt

Combine all ingredients; beat with a wire whisk until smooth. Yield: frosting for about 4 dozen cookies.

Note: Coconut may be tinted by adding a few drops of food coloring to shredded coconut. Place in a jar, and shake until coconut is uniform in color.

BACHELOR BUTTONS

1 cup butter or margarine
1 cup firmly packed brown sugar
1 egg
2 cups all-purpose flour
1 teaspoon baking soda
⅛ teaspoon salt
1 cup chopped black walnuts
1 cup flaked coconut

Cream butter in a large mixing bowl; gradually add sugar, beating until light and fluffy. Add egg; beat well.

Combine flour, soda, and salt; add to creamed mixture, blending well. Stir in walnuts and coconut.

Shape dough into 1-inch balls. Place 2 inches apart on ungreased cookie sheets, and press center of each cookie with finger to form button. Bake at 400° for 10 minutes. Remove to wire racks to cool. Yield: 5 dozen.

COCONUT GUMDROP COOKIES

1 cup shortening
1 cup sugar
1 cup firmly packed dark brown
   sugar
2 eggs, well beaten
1 teaspoon vanilla extract
2 cups all-purpose flour
1 teaspoon baking powder
1 teaspoon baking soda
¼ teaspoon salt
1 cup flaked coconut
2 cups quick-cooking or regular
   oats, uncooked
1 cup chopped pecans
1 cup chopped gumdrops

Cream shortening in a large mixing bowl; gradually add sugar, beating well. Add eggs; beat well. Stir in vanilla.

Sift together flour, baking powder, soda, and salt; add to creamed mixture, mixing well. Stir in coconut, oats, pecans, and gumdrops.

Shape dough into 1-inch balls; place 2 inches apart on greased cookie sheets. Gently flatten balls, using a fork dipped in flour. Bake at 375° for 10 minutes. Remove to wire racks to cool. Yield: 5 dozen.

CHRISTMAS CRUNCHIES

½ cup butter or margarine,
    softened
½ cup sugar
½ cup firmly packed brown
    sugar
1 egg
½ teaspoon vanilla extract
1 cup all-purpose flour
¼ teaspoon baking powder
½ teaspoon baking soda
¼ teaspoon salt
1 cup regular oats, uncooked
1 cup corn flakes
½ cup shredded coconut
½ cup coarsely chopped pecans

Cream butter; add sugar, beating well. Add egg; beat well. Stir in vanilla.

Combine flour, baking powder, soda, and salt in a small mixing bowl; add to creamed mixture, beating well. Stir in oats, corn flakes, coconut, and pecans.

Shape dough into 1-inch balls; place 2 inches apart on lightly greased cookie sheets. Bake at 350° for 10 to 12 minutes. Remove to wire racks to cool. Yield: about 3½ dozen.

CREOLE PORCUPINES

3 tablespoons butter, melted
1 cup firmly packed brown
    sugar
2 eggs, well beaten
1½ cups chopped pecans
1 cup chopped dates
3 cups shredded coconut,
    divided

Cream butter in a large mixing bowl; add sugar, beating well. Add eggs, beating well. Stir in pecans, dates, and 1 cup coconut.

Shape dough into ¾-inch balls, and roll in remaining coconut. Place 2 inches apart on greased cookie sheets. Bake at 300° for 25 minutes or until lightly browned. Remove to wire racks to cool. Yield: about 4 dozen.

LEMON DELIGHTS

1 cup butter, softened
⅓ cup sifted powdered sugar
1¼ cups all-purpose flour
¾ cup cornstarch
½ cup finely chopped pecans
    Lemon Frosting

Cream butter in a medium mixing bowl; gradually add sugar, beating until light and fluffy. Add flour and cornstarch; mix well. Cover and chill at least 1 hour.

Shape dough into 1-inch balls, and roll in pecans to coat lightly. Gently flatten each cookie with bottom of a glass dipped in flour. Place on ungreased cookie sheets. Bake at 350° for 12 to 14 minutes. Remove to wire racks to cool. Spread Lemon Frosting evenly over each cookie. Yield: 2½ dozen.

Lemon Frosting:

1½ cups sifted powdered
    sugar
1½ teaspoons butter or margarine,
    softened
1 tablespoon plus 1½ teaspoons
    lemon juice

Combine sugar, butter, and lemon juice; beat with a wire whisk until smooth. Yield: frosting for 2½ dozen cookies.

LEMON PRALINE COOKIES

¾ cup butter or margarine,
    softened
2 cups firmly packed brown
    sugar
2 eggs
2 teaspoons grated lemon
    rind
1 tablespoon lemon juice
2 cups all-purpose flour
1 cup finely chopped pecans

Cream butter in a medium mixing bowl; gradually add sugar, beating well.

Add eggs, lemon rind, and juice; beat until well blended. Add flour and pecans, stirring well. Cover and refrigerate overnight.

Shape dough into 1-inch balls; place 3 inches apart on greased cookie sheets. Bake at 375° for 6 to 8 minutes. Cool slightly on cookie sheets; remove to wire racks to cool completely. Yield: about 3 dozen.

LEMON CHEESE LOGS

1 cup butter or margarine,
    softened
1 (3-ounce) package cream cheese,
    softened
1 cup sugar
1 egg yolk
2½ cups all-purpose flour
½ teaspoon salt
½ teaspoon grated lemon rind
1 cup finely chopped walnuts
1 (6-ounce) package semisweet
    chocolate morsels, melted
    Decorator candies

Cream butter and cream cheese in a large mixing bowl; gradually add sugar, beating until light and fluffy. Add egg yolk, beating well. Stir in flour, salt, lemon rind, and walnuts; mix well. Cover and chill at least 2 hours.

Shape dough by tablespoonfuls into 2-inch logs; place on ungreased baking sheets. Bake at 325° for 12 minutes or until lightly browned. Remove to wire racks to cool.

Dip one end of each log in melted chocolate, and sprinkle with decorator candies. Place on wire racks until chocolate sets. Store between layers of waxed paper in airtight containers. Yield: 12 dozen.

Note: These cookies freeze well.

ORANGE-WALNUT COOKIES

½ cup butter or margarine
⅓ cup sugar
1 egg, separated
½ teaspoon vanilla extract
1 tablespoon grated orange rind
1 tablespoon grated lemon rind
1 cup all-purpose flour
    Dash of salt
2 cups chopped walnuts

Cream butter in a large mixing bowl; gradually add sugar, beating until light and fluffy. Add egg yolk; beat well. Stir in vanilla, orange rind, and lemon rind. Add flour and salt, blending well.

Shape dough into ¾-inch balls; coat with unbeaten egg white, and roll in walnuts. Place 2 inches apart on well-greased cookie sheets; press to flatten slightly. Bake at 350° for 12 minutes or until lightly browned. Remove to wire racks to cool. Store in airtight containers. Yield: 2½ dozen.

RASPBERRY COOKIES

2 cups butter or margarine,
    softened
½ cup sugar
2 teaspoons almond extract
4 cups all-purpose flour
1 teaspoon salt
    Sesame seeds
    Raspberry preserves

Cream butter in a large mixing bowl; gradually add sugar, beating until light and fluffy. Add almond extract, flour, and salt; mix well. Wrap dough in plastic wrap, and chill 1 hour.

Shape dough into 1-inch balls, and roll in sesame seeds. Place 2 inches apart on lightly greased cookie sheets. Flatten cookies slightly, and indent centers with thumb; fill centers with raspberry preserves. Bake at 400° for 12 to 15 minutes. Remove to wire racks to cool. Store in airtight containers. Yield: about 5 dozen.

BRAZIL NUT STICKS

2 eggs
2 cups firmly packed brown
    sugar
1 teaspoon vanilla extract
1¾ cups all-purpose flour
½ teaspoon baking powder
½ teaspoon salt
1 pound ground Brazil nuts
    Sifted powdered sugar
    (optional)

Beat eggs in large bowl until thick and lemon colored; gradually add brown sugar, beating well after each addition. Stir in vanilla.

Sift together flour, baking powder, and salt in a medium mixing bowl; stir in Brazil nuts to coat well. Add to creamed mixture, blending well. Chill several hours.

Shape dough by teaspoonfuls into 2-inch rolls; place 2 inches apart on well-greased cookie sheets. Bake at 350° for 12 to 15 minutes. Roll in powdered sugar, if desired. Yield: about 12½ dozen.

Note: Ends of baked sticks may be dipped in melted semisweet chocolate morsels and coated with ground nuts.

GIANT PEANUT BUTTER COOKIES

½ cup butter or margarine,
    softened
1 cup sugar
1 cup plus 2 tablespoons firmly
    packed brown sugar
3 eggs
2 cups peanut butter
¼ teaspoon vanilla
    extract
¾ teaspoon light corn syrup
4½ cups regular oats,
    uncooked
2 teaspoons baking soda
¼ teaspoon salt
1 cup candy-coated peanut butter
    pieces
1 cup chopped walnuts

Cream butter in a large mixing bowl; gradually add sugar, beating well. Add eggs, peanut butter, vanilla, and syrup; beat well. Add oats, soda, and salt; stirring well. Stir in peanut butter pieces and walnuts. (Batter will be stiff.)

Spoon dough, ¼ cup at a time, 4 inches apart onto lightly greased cookie sheets; press each into a 3-inch circle. Bake at 350° for 12 to 15 minutes. (Centers of cookies will be slightly soft.) Cool slightly on cookie sheets; remove to wire racks. Yield: 2½ dozen.

EASY PEANUT BUTTER COOKIES

¼ cup shortening
¼ cup butter
½ cup peanut butter
½ cup sugar
½ cup firmly packed brown
    sugar
1 egg
1½ cups all-purpose flour
½ teaspoon baking powder
¾ teaspoon baking soda
¼ teaspoon salt

Cream shortening, butter, and peanut butter in a large mixing bowl; gradually add sugar, beating until light and fluffy. Add egg; beat well.

Sift together flour, baking powder, soda, and salt in a medium mixing bowl. Add to creamed mixture, blending well. Chill thoroughly.

Shape dough into 1½-inch balls. Place 3 inches apart on lightly greased cookie sheets. Gently flatten with a fork dipped in flour, making a crisscross pattern on each. Bake at 375° for 10 to 12 minutes. Remove to wire racks to cool. Yield: about 3 dozen.

PEANUT BUTTER COOKIES

1 cup shortening
1 cup sugar
1 cup firmly packed dark brown
   sugar
2 eggs
1 cup peanut butter
1 teaspoon vanilla extract
3 cups all-purpose flour
¾ teaspoon baking soda

Cream shortening in a large mixing bowl; gradually add sugar, beating well. Add eggs; beat well. Add peanut butter and vanilla; blend well. Add flour and soda, blending well.

Shape dough into 1-inch balls; place 3 inches apart on greased cookie sheets, and gently flatten with a fork dipped in flour. Bake at 350° for 10 to 12 minutes. Remove to wire racks to cool. Yield: 6 dozen.

PEANUT CRUNCH COOKIES

½ cup butter or margarine
½ cup chunky peanut butter
½ cup sugar
½ cup firmly packed brown sugar
1 egg, beaten
1½ cups all-purpose flour
½ teaspoon baking powder
¾ teaspoon baking soda
¼ teaspoon salt

Cream butter and peanut butter; gradually add sugar, beating until light and fluffy. Add egg; beat well.

Sift together flour, baking powder, soda, and salt in a medium mixing bowl. Add to creamed mixture; mix well.

Shape dough into ¾-inch balls; place 3 inches apart on ungreased cookie sheets. Gently flatten with a fork dipped in flour. Bake at 375° for 10 to 12 minutes. Remove to wire racks to cool. Yield: 4 dozen.

PEANUT BUTTER ROUNDUPS

1 cup shortening
¾ cup sugar
1 cup firmly packed brown sugar
2 eggs
1 cup peanut butter
2 cups all-purpose flour
2 teaspoons baking soda
½ teaspoon salt
1 cup quick-cooking or regular
   oats, uncooked

Cream shortening in a large mixing bowl; gradually add sugar, beating until light and fluffy. Add eggs and peanut butter; beat well.

Sift together flour, soda, and salt in a medium mixing bowl. Add to creamed mixture; mix well. Stir in oats. Shape dough into 1-inch balls; place 3 inches apart on ungreased cookie sheets. Gently flatten with a fork dipped in flour, making a crisscross pattern on each. Bake at 350° for 8 to 10 minutes. Remove to wire racks to cool. Yield: 6 dozen.

ARKANSAS TRAVELERS

1 cup butter or margarine
1 cup sugar
1 cup firmly packed brown sugar
2 eggs
1 teaspoon vanilla extract
1 cup peanut butter
3 cups all-purpose flour
2 teaspoons baking powder
1 cup chopped dates or pecans
   (optional)

Cream butter in a large mixing bowl; gradually add sugar, beating well. Add eggs; beat well. Stir in vanilla. Add peanut butter, and mix well.

Sift together flour and baking powder; add to creamed mixture. Add dates or pecans, if desired.

Shape dough into ¾-inch balls; place 3 inches apart on greased cookie sheets. Gently flatten with a fork dipped in water. Bake at 375° for 10 to 15 minutes. Remove to wire racks to cool. Yield: about 5 dozen.

LOLLIPOP COOKIES

½ cup shortening, softened
½ cup sugar
½ cup firmly packed brown
    sugar
1 egg
1 teaspoon vanilla
    extract
1 teaspoon water
1 cup all-purpose flour
1 teaspoon baking powder
¼ teaspoon salt
1 cup quick-cooking or regular
    oats, uncooked
Powdered Sugar Frosting
Semisweet chocolate
    morsels
Gumdrops
Cinnamon candies
Tinted flaked coconut

Cream shortening in a large mixing bowl; gradually add sugar, beating well. Add egg; beat well. Stir in vanilla and water.

Sift together flour, baking powder, and salt in a medium mixing bowl. Gradually add to creamed mixture, beating until mixture is smooth. Stir in oats, blending well.

Shape dough into 1-inch balls; place 2 inches apart on ungreased cookie sheets, and flatten with bottom of a glass dipped in flour. Insert a wooden skewer in top of each. Bake at 350° for 11 to 12 minutes. Remove to wire racks to cool. Using Powdered Sugar Frosting, attach semisweet chocolate morsels for eyes, gumdrops for nose, cinnamon candies for mouth, and tinted coconut for hair. Yield: 2 dozen.

Powdered Sugar Frosting:

½ cup powdered sugar
  Hot water

Sift powdered sugar into a small mixing bowl. Add enough hot water to yield desired spreading consistency, beating with a wire whisk until smooth. Yield: frosting for 2 dozen cookies.

CANDY CANE COOKIES

⅓ cup finely crushed
    peppermint candy
⅓ cup sugar
½ cup shortening
½ cup butter or margarine,
    softened
1 cup sifted powdered
    sugar
1 egg, lightly beaten
1 teaspoon vanilla extract
1 teaspoon almond extract
2½ cups all-purpose flour
1 teaspoon salt
½ teaspoon red food
    coloring

Combine candy and ⅓ cup sugar in a small mixing bowl, mixing well. Set aside.

Cream shortening and butter in a large mixing bowl; gradually add 1 cup sugar, beating until light and fluffy. Add egg; beat well. Stir in flavorings. Add flour and salt; mix well.

Divide dough in half; tint half of dough with food coloring. Shape tinted and plain dough by teaspoonfuls into 4½-inch rolls on a lightly floured surface. Place a tinted and a plain roll side by side; carefully twist together. Curve one end down to resemble a cane. Repeat procedure with remaining dough. Place cookies on ungreased cookie sheets; bake at 375° for 9 minutes or just until edges begin to brown. Remove cookies from cookie sheets while warm; immediately coat with reserved candy mixture. Cool completely on wire racks. Yield: about 4 dozen.

BASIC PRESSED COOKIES

1 cup butter, softened
⅔ cup sugar
1 egg
1 teaspoon almond extract
2½ cups all-purpose flour
½ teaspoon baking powder
⅛ teaspoon salt

Cream butter in a medium mixing bowl; gradually add sugar, beating until light and fluffy. Add egg and almond extract; beat well.

Combine flour, baking powder, and salt in a medium mixing bowl; gradually add to creamed mixture, stirring well. Press dough from a cookie press onto ungreased cookie sheets, using desired shaping discs. Bake at 400° for 6 to 8 minutes. Remove to wire racks to cool. Yield: about 4 dozen.

Note: Dough may be tinted and sprinkled with colored sugar, if desired.

SPRITZ COOKIES

1 cup shortening
¾ cup sugar
1 egg
1 teaspoon vanilla extract
2¼ cups all-purpose flour
½ teaspoon baking powder
¼ teaspoon salt
   Frosting (recipe follows)

Cream shortening in a medium mixing bowl; gradually add sugar, beating until light and fluffy. Add egg and vanilla, beating well.

Sift together flour, baking powder, and salt in a medium mixing bowl; add to creamed mixture, stirring well.

Press dough from a cookie press 2 inches apart onto ungreased cookie sheets, using desired shaping discs. Bake at 350° for 12 to 15 minutes. Remove to wire racks to cool.

Spoon frosting into a pastry bag fitted with a star tip; decorate each cookie as desired. Yield: about 5½ dozen.

Frosting:

⅔ cup shortening
¼ teaspoon salt
½ teaspoon vanilla or almond extract
1 (16-ounce) package powdered sugar, sifted
⅓ cup water
   Paste food coloring (optional)

Combine shortening, salt, and desired flavoring in a medium mixing bowl; beat at medium speed of an electric mixer until well blended. Add sugar alternately with water, beginning and ending with sugar; beat constantly at low speed until smooth. Beat an additional 8 minutes at medium speed. Color portions of frosting with paste food coloring, if desired. Yield: frosting for about 5½ dozen cookies.

CREAM CHEESE SPRITZ COOKIES

1 cup butter or margarine, softened
1 (8-ounce) package cream cheese, softened
⅔ cup sugar
1 teaspoon vanilla extract
2 cups all-purpose flour
   Dash of salt
   Red and green decorator sugar crystals (optional)
   Assorted candies and sprinkles (optional)

Cream together butter and cream cheese in a large mixing bowl; gradually add sugar, beating until light and fluffy. Stir in vanilla.

Combine flour and salt; gradually add to creamed mixture, beating until well blended. Shape dough into a ball, and chill thoroughly.

Press dough from a cookie press 2 inches apart onto ungreased cookie sheets, using desired shaping discs. Sprinkle with sugar crystals, if desired. Bake at 400° for 8 to 10 minutes or until very lightly browned. Remove to wire racks to cool. Decorate with assorted candies and sprinkles, if desired. Yield: about 4 dozen.

DOUBLE-DIP NUT FINGERS

1¼ cups butter or margarine,
　　softened
　¾ cup sugar
　1 egg
　2 teaspoons grated orange
　　rind
3¼ cups all-purpose flour
　½ teaspoon baking powder
　¼ teaspoon salt
　1 (6-ounce) package semisweet
　　chocolate morsels
　¼ cup plus 2 tablespoons whipping
　　cream
　　Chopped pecans
　　Shredded coconut
　　Colored sugar

Cream butter in a large mixing bowl;
gradually add sugar, beating until light
and fluffy. Add egg and orange rind;
beat well.

Sift together flour, baking powder,
and salt in a medium mixing bowl; add
to creamed mixture, mixing well.

Use a cookie press fitted with a star
disc to shape dough into 3-inch-long
fingers on ungreased cookie sheets.
Bake at 400° for 5 to 7 minutes. Remove
to wire racks to cool.

Melt chocolate morsels in top of a double boiler over simmering water. Remove
from heat, and cool slightly. Gradually
add whipping cream, stirring until well
blended.

Dip ends of cookies in chocolate, cov-
ering ½ inch on each end. Sprinkle ends
with pecans, coconut, or colored sugar.
Place on wire racks until chocolate sets.
Yield: about 7 dozen.

CHOCOLATE KISS COOKIES

1¼ cups butter or margarine,
　　softened
　1 cup sugar
　2 eggs
　½ teaspoon vanilla extract
3¼ cups all-purpose flour
　1 (14-ounce) package chocolate
　　kiss candies

Cream butter; gradually add sugar,
beating until light and fluffy. Add eggs
and vanilla; blend well. Stir in flour.

Press dough from a cookie press 2
inches apart onto ungreased cookie
sheets, using a star- or daisy-shaped
disc. Bake at 375° for 10 minutes. Press
a chocolate kiss in center of each warm
cookie, point side up. Remove to wire
racks to cool. Yield: 6 dozen.

BLACK-EYED SUSANS

　½ cup butter or margarine,
　　softened
　½ cup sugar
　½ cup firmly packed brown sugar
　1 egg
　1 tablespoon plus 1½ teaspoons
　　warm water
　1 teaspoon vanilla extract
　1 cup peanut butter
1½ cups all-purpose flour
　½ teaspoon baking soda
　½ teaspoon salt
　½ cup semisweet chocolate
　　morsels

Cream butter; gradually add sugar,
beating well. Add egg, warm water, vanilla, and peanut butter; beat well.

Combine flour, soda, and salt in a
small mixing bowl; add to creamed mixture, mixing well. Press dough from a
cookie press 2 inches apart onto lightly
greased cookie sheets, using a flower-
shaped disc. Place a chocolate morsel in
center of each flower shape.

Bake at 350° for 8 minutes or until
lightly browned. Remove to wire racks to
cool. Chill 30 minutes or until chocolate
center hardens. Yield: about 10 dozen.

MADELEINES

　2 eggs
　⅛ teaspoon salt
　⅓ cup sugar
　½ cup all-purpose flour
　1 teaspoon grated lemon rind
　½ cup butter, melted and cooled
　　Sifted powdered sugar

Combine eggs and salt in a large mixing bowl, beating at medium speed of an electric mixer. Gradually add ⅓ cup sugar; beat at high speed 15 minutes or until thick and lemon colored. Fold in flour, 2 tablespoons at a time, and lemon rind. Fold in butter, 1 tablespoon at a time. Spoon 1 tablespoon batter into greased and floured madeleine molds. Bake at 400° for 8 to 10 minutes or until lightly browned. Remove from molds, and cool flat side down on wire racks. Sprinkle with powdered sugar. Store in airtight containers. Yield: 1 dozen.

ROLLED SWEET WAFERS

½ cup butter or margarine,
   softened
⅔ cup sugar
1 egg
1 cup all-purpose flour
½ cup milk
1 teaspoon vanilla extract
  Vegetable oil

Cream butter in a medium mixing bowl; gradually add sugar, beating until light and fluffy. Add egg; beat well. Add flour alternately with milk, beginning and ending with flour. Mix well after each addition. Stir in vanilla.

Brush pizelle or waffle iron with oil; preheat iron 2 mintues. Place 1 heaping teaspoon batter in center of iron; close iron, and bake 1 minute or until lightly browned. Remove wafer, and quickly roll up; cool on a wire rack. Repeat baking procedure with remaining batter. Store wafers in an airtight container. Yield: about 2½ dozen.

Note: These wafers are delicious served with ice cream.

FRENCH COOKIES

5 eggs, separated
6¾ cups all-purpose flour
2 cups sugar
2 cups firmly packed brown
   sugar
⅛ teaspoon baking powder
2 cups butter, melted
1 teaspoon vanilla extract

Beat egg yolks in a small mixing bowl until thick and lemon colored; set aside.

Beat egg whites (at room temperature) in a medium mixing bowl until foamy; set aside.

Combine flour, sugar, and baking powder in a large mixing bowl; mix well. Stir in butter, reserved egg yolks, and vanilla. Fold in egg whites, blending well. Cover and refrigerate overnight.

Shape dough into 1-inch balls. Bake, a few at a time, in a preheated lightly oiled waffle iron 1 minute or until golden brown. Cool on wire racks, and store in airtight containers. Yield: about 11 dozen.

Note: Dough may also be shaped into balls and frozen.

FOREIGN COOKIES

ALSATIAN PLUM COOKIES

¼ cup plus 2 tablespoons
 shortening
2 cups sugar
3 eggs
1 (8-ounce) package pitted
 dates
1½ cups chopped pecans
1½ cups raisins
½ teaspoon ground cinnamon
½ teaspoon ground nutmeg
½ teaspoon ground cloves
¼ teaspoon salt
1 teaspoon baking soda
1 tablespoon half-and-half
4 cups all-purpose flour

Cream shortening in a large mixing bowl; gradually add sugar, beating well. Add eggs, one at a time, beating well after each addition.

Grind together dates, pecans, and raisins in a medium mixing bowl. Add fruit mixture, spices, and salt to creamed mixture, stirring well. Dissolve soda in half-and-half; add to fruit mixture, stirring until well blended. Add flour, blending well. (Dough will be stiff.) Divide dough into thirds; shape each portion into a roll, 1½ inches in diameter. Wrap rolls in waxed paper, and chill overnight or until firm.

Remove waxed paper, and cut rolls into ¼-inch slices; place 2 inches apart on ungreased cookie sheets. Bake at 350° for 10 to 12 minutes. Remove to wire racks to cool. Store in airtight containers. Yield: 10 dozen.

BIZCOCHOS

2 cups lard, softened
2 cups sugar, divided
2 egg yolks
5 cups all-purpose
 flour
3 tablespoons ground cinnamon,
 divided
1 tablespoon anise seeds
1 cup Sauterne or other sweet
 wine

Cream lard in a large mixing bowl; gradually add 1 cup sugar, beating until light and fluffy. Add egg yolks, beating until well blended.

Combine flour, 1 tablespoon cinnamon, and anise in a large mixing bowl; stir well. Gradually add to creamed mixture alternately with wine, beginning and ending with flour mixture. Divide dough into fourths. Cover and chill at least 1 hour.

Roll one portion of dough to ½-inch thickness on a lightly floured surface. Cut into assorted shapes, using 2-inch cookie cutters. Place on greased baking sheets. Bake at 350° for 12 minutes or until edges are lightly browned. Cool slightly on cookie sheets.

Combine remaining 1 cup sugar and 2 tablespoons cinnamon in a small mixing bowl; dredge warm cookies in mixture. Cool completely on wire racks. Repeat procedure with remaining dough and cinnamon-sugar mixture. Store in airtight containers. Yield: about 6 dozen.

DUTCH FRUIT COOKIES

1 cup butter or margarine
⅔ cup sugar
½ cup light corn syrup
1 egg, beaten
1 cup chopped mixed candied fruit
1 cup chopped toasted blanched
   almonds
1 teaspoon vanilla extract
3 cups all-purpose flour
¼ teaspoon soda
¼ teaspoon salt
1 teaspoon ground cardamom
   seeds
½ teaspoon ground cloves
½ teaspoon ground cinnamon
½ teaspoon ground allspice
½ teaspoon ground nutmeg

Cream butter in a large mixing bowl; gradually add sugar and syrup, beating until light and fluffy. Add egg; blend well. Stir in fruit, almonds, and vanilla.

Sift together flour, soda, salt, and spices in a medium mixing bowl; add to creamed mixture, mixing well. Shape dough into 2 rolls, 2 inches in diameter. Wrap in waxed paper; chill.

Remove waxed paper, and cut rolls into ¼-inch slices. Place 2 inches apart on ungreased cookie sheets. Bake at 400° for 8 to 10 minutes or until edges are browned. Remove to wire racks to cool. Yield: about 5 dozen.

FATTIGMANDS BAKKELSE

¾ cup sugar
2 eggs
8 egg yolks
3 tablespoons brandy
1 cup whipping cream
5 cups all-purpose flour
1 teaspoon ground cardamom
   Vegetable oil
   Powdered sugar

Combine ¾ cup sugar, eggs, egg yolks, and brandy; beat until thick and lemon colored. Gradually add whipping cream; beat well.

Sift together flour and cardamom; add to sugar mixture, ½ cup at a time, stirring well after each addition. Cover and refrigerate overnight.

Turn out a small portion of dough onto a lightly floured surface; roll to ⅛-inch thickness. Cut into 3- x 2-inch diamonds; make a ¾-inch lengthwise slit in center of each, and gently pull one corner through as far as possible without tearing. Drop 3 to 4 at a time into 4 inches of hot oil (375°). Cook, turning once, 2 minutes or until golden brown. Drain on paper towels; sift powdered sugar over tops of cookies. Repeat procedure with remaining dough. Yield: 6 dozen.

GRECIAN DATE ROLLS

¾ cup butter or margarine,
   softened
1 cup sugar, divided
1 egg yolk
3 cups all-purpose flour
½ cup milk
2 (8-ounce) packages pitted dates
1 cup chopped pecans
2 egg whites, lightly beaten

Cream butter; gradually add ½ cup sugar, beating until light and fluffy. Add egg yolk; beat well. Gradually add flour to creamed mixture alternately with milk, beginning and ending with flour; beat well after each addition. Divide dough into thirds; chill 1 hour.

Roll one portion of dough to ⅛-inch thickness between 2 sheets of waxed paper; keep remaining dough chilled until ready to use. Remove top layer of waxed paper, and cut dough into 2-inch squares. Place 1 date in center of each square; fold and press dough around date. Combine pecans and remaining sugar; stir well. Dip cookies in egg whites; roll in pecan mixture.

Place 2 inches apart on greased cookie sheets. Bake at 350° for 20 minutes or until lightly browned. Remove to wire racks to cool. Repeat procedure with remaining dough. Yield: 6½ dozen.

GREEK HOLIDAY COOKIES

  1 (6-ounce) jar maraschino
    cherries, undrained
  1 cup chopped pecans
  ¼ cup quince jelly
  ¼ teaspoon ground cinnamon
1½ teaspoons Cognac
  2 cups all-purpose flour
  ½ teaspoon salt
  ¾ cup shortening
  5 to 6 tablespoons cold water
    Marachino cherry halves,
      drained
  ½ cup sugar
  1 cup water
  2 tablespoons honey
1½ teaspoons lemon juice

Drain cherries, reserving liquid, and chop. Combine chopped cherries, reserved liquid, chopped pecans, jelly, cinnamon, and Cognac in a medium mixing bowl; mix until thoroughly blended. Set aside.

Combine flour and salt in a medium mixing bowl; cut in shortening with a pastry blender until mixture resembles coarse meal. Sprinkle 5 to 6 tablespoons water evenly over surface of flour mixture; stir with a fork until dry ingredients are moistened. Shape dough into a ball; chill.

Roll half of pastry to ⅛-inch thickness on a lightly floured surface; cut with a 3-inch round cutter. Place a heaping teaspoonful of reserved cherry mixture in center of each cookie; overlap sides, forming a cylinder. Insert a cherry half in each open end. Place 2 inches apart on lightly greased cookie sheets. Repeat procedure with remaining dough. Bake at 400° for 20 to 25 minutes or until lightly browned. Remove to wire racks to cool completely.

Combine sugar, 1 cup water, honey, and lemon juice in a saucepan; bring to a boil. Reduce heat; simmer, uncovered, 15 minutes, stirring occasionally. Cool glaze to room temperature; drizzle over cookies. Let dry completely before serving. Store in airtight containers. Yield: about 2 dozen.

GERMAN CHRISTMAS COOKIES

  1 cup honey
  ¾ cup firmly packed brown sugar
  1 egg, beaten
  1 tablespoon lemon juice
2¼ cups all-purpose flour
  ½ teaspoon baking soda
  ½ teaspoon salt
  ¾ teaspoon ground cinnamon
  ½ teaspoon ground allspice
  ½ teaspoon ground nutmeg
  ¼ teaspoon ground cloves
  ¼ cup finely chopped almonds
  ⅓ cup finely chopped candied
      citron
    Candied red cherry halves
    Whole blanched almonds
  1 cup plus 2 tablespoons sifted
      powdered sugar
  ¼ cup plus 1 tablespoon rum or
      water

Heat honey in a medium saucepan just until warm. Add brown sugar, egg, and lemon juice, stirring well.

Sift together flour, soda, salt, and spices in a large mixing bowl. Add honey mixture, almonds, and citron; stir until blended. Divide dough into fourths; cover and chill overnight.

Roll one portion of dough to ¼-inch thickness on a heavily floured surface; keep remaining dough chilled until ready to use. Cut dough with a 2½-inch round cutter; place 2 inches apart on a greased cookie sheet. Gently press a candied cherry half in center of each, and arrange 5 almonds radiating from center of each cherry. Bake at 375° for 12 minutes or until golden brown. Remove to wire racks.

Combine powdered sugar and rum; stir until blended. Brush rum mixture evenly over warm cookies. Let cool completely. Repeat procedure with remaining dough. Store in an airtight container. Yield: about 2 dozen.

Note: When first baked, cookies are hard and crunchy. They are typically stored in an airtight container for 2 weeks to soften, although they may be eaten earlier, if desired.

ITALIAN HOLIDAY COOKIES

½ cup butter or margarine
⅓ cup sugar
1 egg yolk
¼ teaspoon vanilla extract
1 cup plus 2 tablespoons
   all-purpose flour
½ teaspoon salt
1 egg white, lightly beaten
1 cup flaked coconut
Preserves

Cream butter in a large mixing bowl; gradually add sugar, beating until light and fluffy. Add egg yolk and vanilla, and beat well.

Sift together flour and salt; gradually add to creamed mixture, stirring well. Chill dough until easy to handle.

Shape dough into 1-inch balls; dip each in egg white, and roll in coconut. Place 2 inches apart on lightly greased cookie sheets; press top of each ball gently with thumb to make an indentation. Bake at 300° for 20 to 25 minutes. Remove to wire racks to cool; fill centers with preserves. Yield: 3½ dozen.

JAM KOLACHES

½ cup butter or margarine,
   softened
1 (3-ounce) package cream cheese,
   softened
1¼ cups all-purpose flour
   About ¼ cup strawberry jam
¼ cup sifted powdered sugar

Cream butter and cream cheese in a medium mixing bowl; beat until light and fluffy. Add flour, mixing well.

Roll dough to ⅛-inch thickness on a lightly floured surface; cut with a 2-inch round cutter. Place 2 inches apart on lightly greased cookie sheets. Spoon ¼ teaspoon jam on each cookie; fold opposite sides together, slightly overlapping edges. Bake at 375° for 15 minutes. Remove to wire racks to cool, and sprinkle with powdered sugar. Yield: about 2 dozen.

LEBKUCHEN BARS

1 egg, beaten
1 cup firmly packed brown sugar
½ cup molasses
½ cup honey
3½ cups all-purpose flour
½ teaspoon baking soda
⅛ teaspoon salt
1 teaspoon ground cinnamon
1 teaspoon ground nutmeg
1 teaspoon ground cloves
¾ cup chopped candied cherries
½ cup toasted slivered almonds
Lemon Frosting

Combine egg and brown sugar in a large mixing bowl; mix well. Stir in molasses and honey, and set aside.

Combine flour, soda, salt, and spices in a medium mixing bowl. Combine 1 cup flour mixture, cherries, and almonds, tossing to coat; set aside. Add remaining flour mixture to molasses mixture, stirring well; fold in cherry and almond mixture.

Press dough into a greased 15- x 10- x 1-inch jellyroll pan. Bake at 300° for 40 minutes. Cool in pan on a wire rack. Spread Lemon Frosting evenly over surface; cut into 3- x 1-inch bars. Yield: about 4 dozen.

Lemon Frosting:

1 egg white, beaten
2 cups sifted powdered sugar
½ teaspoon grated lemon rind
1 tablespoon lemon juice
⅛ teaspoon salt

Combine all ingredients; beat with a wire whisk until smooth. Yield: frosting for about 4 dozen bars.

NÜRNBERGER LEBKUCHEN

3 cups honey
2¼ cups firmly packed brown sugar
3 eggs, beaten
1 tablespoon grated lemon rind
3 tablespoons lemon juice
8¼ cups all-purpose flour
1½ teaspoons baking soda
1 tablespoon ground cinnamon
1½ teaspoons ground allspice
1½ teaspoons ground nutmeg
1 teaspoon ground cloves
1 cup diced candied citron
1 cup chopped pecans
   Sliced almonds
   Glaze (recipe follows)

Bring honey to a boil in a large Dutch oven; remove from heat, and cool slightly. Stir in sugar, beaten eggs, lemon rind, and juice.

Combine flour, soda, and spices in a large mixing bowl; gradually add to honey mixture, stirring well. Stir in citron and pecans, blending well. Cover and chill overnight.

Shape dough into 1-inch balls; place 2 inches apart on greased cookie sheets. Gently press balls to ¼-inch thickness with bottom of a glass dipped in cool water. Gently press an almond slice in center of each cookie. Bake at 400° for 10 minutes. Remove cookie sheets from oven. Brush glaze over cookies, and remove to wire racks to cool. Yield: about 14 dozen.

Glaze:

1½ cups sugar
¾ cup water
⅓ cup sifted powdered sugar

Combine 1½ cups sugar and water in a small heavy saucepan; cook over low heat, stirring until sugar dissolves. Cook over high heat, without stirring, until mixture reaches thread stage (230°). Remove from heat; stir in powdered sugar, mixing well. Place over low heat, if necessary, to maintain basting consistency. Yield: glaze for about 14 dozen cookies.

LANGUES DE CHAT

2 tablespoons unsalted margarine, softened
2 tablespoons sugar
1 egg white
¾ teaspoon vanilla extract
¼ cup unbleached or all-purpose flour

Cream margarine in a small bowl; gradually add sugar, beating until light and fluffy. Add egg white, beating well. Add vanilla and flour, stirring until well blended.

Spoon batter into a pastry bag fitted with a No. 7 round tip. Pipe mixture in 3-inch fingers onto aluminum foil-lined cookie sheets, making ends slightly thicker.

Bake at 425° for 4 to 5 minutes or until edges are lightly browned. Cool 1 minute on baking sheets; remove cookies from cookie sheets, and cool completely on a wire rack. Store in airtight containers. Yield: 1½ dozen.

NORWEGIAN ALMOND COOKIES

¾ cup butter or margarine
½ cup sifted powdered sugar
1 cup finely ground, unblanched almonds
1 teaspoon fresh lemon juice
1 egg
1½ cups all-purpose flour

Cream butter in a large mixing bowl; gradually add sugar, beating until light and fluffy.

Sift almonds through a colander or coarse sieve; add to creamed mixture, mixing until well blended. Add lemon juice and egg, mixing well. Gradually blend in flour, stirring well.

Press dough from a cookie press 2 inches apart onto ungreased cookie sheets, using desired discs. Bake at 400° for 7 to 10 minutes. Remove to wire racks to cool. Store in airtight containers. Yield: 5½ dozen.

PFEFFERNÜSSE

¾ **cup molasses**
¾ **cup honey**
¾ **cup shortening**
4 **cups all-purpose flour**
1 **teaspoon baking soda**
1 **teaspoon salt**
1 **teaspoon ground allspice**
1 **teaspoon ground mace**
½ **teaspoon pepper**
¼ **teaspoon anise seeds, crushed**
1 **egg, beaten**
  Sifted powdered sugar

Combine molasses and honey in a medium saucepan; cook over low heat until thoroughly heated, stirring frequently. Add shortening; stir until well blended. Remove from heat, and set aside to cool.

Combine flour, soda, salt, allspice, mace, pepper, and anise in a large mixing bowl; stir well.

Add egg to cooled molasses mixture, stirring until well blended. Gradually pour into flour mixture, stirring just until dry ingredients are moistened. Allow dough to rest 15 minutes.

Shape dough into 1-inch balls, and place 2 inches apart on greased cookie sheets. Bake at 350° for 10 minutes. Remove from cookie sheets, and roll in powdered sugar. Cool on wire racks. Yield: 9½ dozen.

SCANDINAVIAN WREATH COOKIES

¾ **cup butter, softened**
¾ **cup shortening**
1 **cup plus 2 tablespoons sugar, divided**
2 **eggs**
2 **teaspoons grated orange rind**
4 **cups all-purpose flour**
1 **egg white**

Cream butter and shortening; gradually add 1 cup sugar, beating until light and fluffy. Add 2 eggs; beat well. Stir in orange rind. Gradually add flour, stirring well. Chill dough 1 hour.

Shape dough into 1-inch balls; roll each ball into a 6-inch rope. Tie each rope into a knot, leaving ½-inch ends. Place 2 inches apart on ungreased cookie sheets; set aside.

Beat egg white (at room temperature) until soft peaks form. Gradually add remaining sugar, beating until stiff peaks form. (Do not underbeat.)

Brush meringue over cookies. Bake at 375° for 8 to 10 minutes. Remove to wire racks to cool. Yield: about 8 dozen.

SPECULAAS

1 **cup butter, softened**
1 **cup firmly packed brown sugar**
2 **tablespoons milk**
2 **teaspoons grated orange rind**
2 **cups all-purpose flour**
1 **tablespoon baking powder**
½ **teaspoon salt**
1 **tablespoon ground cinnamon**
1 **teaspoon grated nutmeg**
½ **teaspoon ground cloves**
½ **teaspoon pepper**
½ **teaspoon anise seeds, crushed**
½ **cup blanched whole almonds**

Cream butter in a large mixing bowl; add sugar, and beat until light and fluffy. Add milk and orange rind; beat until well blended.

Sift together remaining ingredients, except almonds, in a medium mixing bowl. Gradually add to creamed mixture, beating well. (Use additional milk, if necessary.)

Divide dough in half; press each portion to ½-inch thickness on greased cookie sheets. Cut each portion into 10 rectangles, and press 4 almonds into each rectangle. Preheat oven to 425° for 7 minutes; reduce heat to 325°, and bake 25 minutes. Cool slightly on cookie sheets; remove to wire racks to cool completely. Break cookies apart, and store in an airtight container. Yield: about 2 dozen.

Note: Wooden cookie molds may be used to press dough into assorted shapes. Omit almonds when following this procedure.

SPANISH HAZLENUT COOKIES

1 cup butter or margarine,
   softened
½ cup sifted powdered sugar
2 cups all-purpose flour
1 cup finely chopped hazlenuts,
   toasted
   Sifted powdered sugar

Cream butter in a large mixing bowl; add ½ cup powdered sugar, beating until light and fluffy. Gradually add flour; beat well. Stir in hazelnuts. Chill 30 minutes.

Shape dough into 1-inch balls; place on ungreased cookie sheets. Bake at 400° for 12 to 14 minutes. Remove immediately from cookie sheets, and roll in powdered sugar. Cool on wire racks. Yield: 3½ dozen.

SPRINGERLE

4 eggs
2 cups sugar
1 tablespoon butter, softened
2 tablespoons anise seeds,
   crushed
3¾ cups all-purpose flour
½ teaspoon baking powder

Beat eggs in a large mixing bowl until thick and lemon colored; gradually add sugar and butter. Continue beating 10 minutes; stir in anise.

Combine flour and baking powder in a medium mixing bowl; stir well. Add to egg mixture, stirring well.

Roll dough to ½-inch thickness on a lightly floured surface. Use a floured cookie mold or springerle rolling pin to imprint dough. Separate cookie squares, using a knife. Place 2 inches apart on well-greased cookie sheets. Let

stand, uncovered, in a cool, dry place 12 hours or overnight to set design.

Bake at 300° for 12 to 15 minutes. Remove from cookie sheets, and cool on wire racks. Store in airtight containers. Yield: about 4½ dozen.

SWEDISH CHRISTMAS COOKIES

½ cup butter or margarine,
   softened
¼ cup sugar
1 egg, separated
1 tablespoon grated orange rind
1 tablespoon lemon juice
2 teaspoons vanilla extract
⅛ teaspoon salt
1 cup cake flour
18 candied cherries, halved

Cream butter in a large mixing bowl; gradually add sugar, beating until light and fluffy. Add egg yolk, and beat 1 minute. Add orange rind, lemon juice, vanilla, and salt; beat thoroughly. Add flour, mixing well. Chill dough 2 hours.

Beat egg white slightly. Shape dough into ¾-inch balls; dip each in egg white, and roll in walnuts. Place 2 inches apart on greased cookie sheets, and flatten slightly with bottom of a glass dipped in flour. Place a cherry half in center of each cookie. Bake at 325° for 20 minutes. Remove to wire racks to cool. Yield: about 3 dozen.

SWEDISH KRINGLER

2 cups all-purpose flour
1 cup butter or margarine
3 tablespoons milk
2 egg yolks
1 egg white
   Sugar or cinnamon-sugar
   mixture

Place flour in a large mixing bowl; cut in butter with a pastry blender until mixture resembles coarse meal. Stir in milk and egg yolks with a fork until dough holds together. Divide dough into fourths, and wrap in waxed paper. Chill at least 1 hour.

Roll one portion of dough into a 10- x 6-inch rectangle on a lightly sugared surface; keep remaining dough chilled until ready to use. Brush surface lightly with egg white. Cut into 10- x ½-inch strips, and shape each like a pretzel on an ungreased cookie sheet. Sprinkle tops with sugar or cinnamon-sugar mixture. Bake at 375° for 12 minutes or until golden brown. Remove to wire racks to cool. Repeat procedure with remaining dough. Yield: 4 dozen.

TUILES WITH ALMONDS

  2 egg whites
 ½ cup sugar
 ½ cup blanched almonds, finely
       ground
 ½ cup all-purpose flour
 ¼ cup butter or margarine, melted
 ½ teaspoon almond extract
 ½ teaspoon vanilla extract

Combine egg whites (at room temperature) and sugar in a medium mixing bowl; beat until foamy. Add ground almonds, flour, butter, and flavorings, stirring until well blended.

Drop by heaping teaspoonfuls 2 inches apart onto three well-greased cookie sheets. Gently flatten cookies with a fork dipped in water. Bake, one sheet of cookies at a time, at 350° for 8 minutes or just until edges are lightly browned. Cool 30 seconds on cookie sheet; immediately loosen cookies, and shape around a rolling pin. (Press gently against the pin for a few seconds.) Slide molded wafers off pin, and place on wire racks to cool completely. Repeat baking and shaping procedure with cookies on remaining cookie sheets. Store cookies in an airtight container. Yield: about 2½ dozen.

ZIMTKRÄNZE

1½ cups butter, softened
1¼ cups sugar, divided
  3 eggs, separated
  3 to 3½ cups all-purpose
       flour
  1 teaspoon ground cinnamon
  1 cup finely chopped pecans

Cream butter in a large mixing bowl; gradually add 1 cup sugar, beating until light and fluffy. Add egg yolks, beating until well blended. Add enough flour to make a stiff dough.

Roll dough to ¼-inch thickness on a floured surface. Cut with a floured 2¾-inch doughnut cutter. Place 2 inches apart on greased cookie sheets, and brush with lightly beaten egg whites. Combine remaining sugar, cinnamon, and pecans; sprinkle over cookies. Bake at 300° for 15 minutes or until lightly browned. Remove to wire racks to cool. Yield: about 5 dozen.

ZIMTSTERNE

  3 egg whites
  1 cup sugar
  2 teaspoons ground cinnamon
  1 teaspoon grated lemon rind
1½ cups ground unblanched
       almonds
  2 tablespoons all-purpose flour
 ⅛ teaspoon salt

Beat egg whites (at room temperature) until soft peaks form; gradually add sugar, cinnamon, and lemon rind, beating until stiff peaks form. Remove ½ cup meringue, and set aside. Fold almonds, flour, and salt into remaining meringue.

Roll small amounts of dough at a time to ¼-inch thickness on a heavily floured surface. Cut with a floured star-shaped cutter. Place cookies 2 inches apart on greased cookie sheets. Frost each cookie lightly with reserved meringue. Bake at 300° for 20 to 30 minutes. Remove to wire racks to cool completely. Yield: about 3 dozen.

INDEX